Sun Tzu's

THE
ART
OF
WAR

Plus ## The Art of
Management

Sun Tzu's Strategy for Managers

Gary Gagliardi

D1718642

"A Brilliant Achievement"

"Gary Gagliardi is to be commended for the clarity and fluidity of his translation of *The Art of War* as well as for his skillful juxtaposition of the content with important issues in the contemporary business world as he focuses on the basic strategies and tactics of effective management... In terms of both Gagliardi's translation and analysis, his is a brilliant achievement."
ROBERT MORRIS, Morris & Associates, *Five-Star Reviews*, Ranked #10 among Amazon and Borders *Top 100 Reviewers*

"Two books in one, this retranslating of Sun Tzu's classic warfare text, *The Art of War*, runs side by side with Gagliardi's application of it to business...Both are excellent guides to their subject."
F. JOHN REH, About.com Guide to Management

This book contains the only award-winning translation of Sun Tzu's *The Art of War*

The Art of War Plus
The Ancient Chinese Revealed

Multicultural Nonfiction
Independent Publishers
Book Award
2003 - Winner

Award Recognition for *Art of War* Strategy Books
by Gary Gagliardi

The Golden Key to Strategy

Psychology/Self-Help
Ben Franklin
Book Award
2006 - Winner

*The Art of War Plus
The Ancient Chinese Revealed*

Multicultural Nonfiction
Independent Publishers
Book Award
2003 - Winner

*Making Money by Speaking:
The Spokesperson Strategy*

Career
Foreword Magazine
Book of the Year
2007 - Finalist

Strategy for Sales Managers

Business
Independent Publishers
Book Award
2006 - Semi-Finalist

*The Warrior Class:
306 Lessons in Strategy*

Self-Help
Foreword Magazine
Book of the Year
2005 - Finalist

Strategy Against Terror

Philosophy
Foreword Magazine
Book of the Year
2005 - Finalist

*The Ancient Bing-fa:
Martial Arts Strategy*

Sports
Foreword Magazine
Book of the Year
2007 - Finalist

*The Art of War
Plus Its Amazing Secrets*

Multicultural Nonfiction
Independent Publishers
Book Award
2005 - Finalist

The Warrior's Apprentice

Youth Nonfiction
Independent Publishers
Book Award
2006 - Semi-Finalist

Published by
Science of Strategy Institute, Clearbridge Publishing
   suntzus.com   scienceofstrategy.org

Fifth Edition
ISBN 978-1-92919448-3 (13-digit) 1-929194-48-x (10-digit)
Also titled in a previous edition: *The Art of War for The Management Warrior*
Copyright 1999, 2000, 2001, 2003, 2004, 2007, 2014 Gary Gagliardi
Registered with Department of Copyrights, Library of Congress
Registration Number TX 5-757-034

Interior and cover graphic design by Dana and Jeff Wincapaw.
Original Chinese calligraphy by Tsai Yung, Green Dragon Arts, www.greendragonarts.com.

Publisher's Cataloging-in-Publication Data
Sun-tzu, 6th cent. B.C.
      [Sun-tzu ping fa, English]
      The art of war for the management warrior/ Sun Tzu and Gary Gagliardi.
      p. 192 cm. 23
      Includes introduction to basic competitive philosophy of Sun Tzu
                1. Management—Study and teaching—U.S. 2. Executives—training of—U.S. 3. Success
in Business. 4. Military art and science - Early works to 1800. I. Gagliardi, Gary 1951— . II. The Art
of War for the Management Warrior
HD31.S764413 2000
658.8 /4 21 —dc19
                                        Library of Congress Catalog Card Number: 00-100175

Science of Strategy Institute/Clearbridge Publishing
2829 Linkview Dr. Las Vegas, NV, 89134
Phone: (702) 721-9631
garyg@suntzus.com
scienceofstrategy.org

Sun Tzu's
THE
ART
OF
WAR

孫子兵法

Plus
The Art of Management
Sun Tzu's Strategy for Managers

by Gary Gagliardi

Science of Strategy Institute
Clearbridge Publishing

Contents

The Art of War Plus
The Art of Management

Foreword

Using Management Strategy

This is a work of translation, not only from the ancient Chinese to English, but from a military terminology to the language of modern management. It works because Sun Tzu wrote about competitive strategy as a battle of minds not weapons. However, as defined by Sun Tzu, competitive strategy is not a system of strategic planning as often envisioned by managers. Planning, in the sense of prioritizing a list of activities, works in controlled environments where you can know how others will respond to your decisions. Competitive strategy works in environments where your decisions collide with the decisions of others, creating conditions that no one planned.

Most managers are confused about the competition. This confusion often arises from two false dichotomies. The first is between competition and cooperation, thinking that since cooperation means working together, competition means working against others. The second false dichotomy is between competition and production, thinking that because production is productive, competition must be destructive. What people fail to see is that competition is essential to both cooperation and production.

Competition exists everywhere there are comparisons among alternative choices. All alternatives choices are "at war" with each other in the sense Sun Tzu used the idea. To put it more nicely, alternatives are in competition with each other. Cooperation requires

競 (孫子兵法 vertical characters in left margin)

competition because we must choose our partners. So potential partners are in competition with each other. Production requires competition because we must choose what to produce, which designs to use, what manufacturing methods to use, which suppliers to use, how to construct the supply chain, and so on. All these alternatives are in competition with each other.

The point of Sun Tzu's work is that, although competition, cooperation, and production all work together to produce value, they demand very different skill sets. Good competitive decisions are not made in the same way that good planning decisions are made. While planning depends on prioritization and organization, competitive decisions depend on agility and positioning, moving quickly and decisively though a shifting kaleidoscope of choices.

Sun Tzu taught that in making these competitive choices, success is not a matter of winning fights with other people. Instead success depends on building and advancing strategic positions. A "position" is defined by Sun Tzu as what people actually compare in making competitive choices. The basis of conflict in competition is trying to weaken opposing positions. Sun Tzu's taught that conflict is inherently destructive, weaken the positions of everyone involved.

The focus of Sun Tzu's system is to create positions that others cannot attack and that ideally they want to join. Sun Tzu teaches that a general who fights a hundred battles and wins a hundred battles is not a good general. A good general is one who finds a way to win without fighting a single battle. Strategy teaches that you win by building the right positions and advancing those positions while avoiding conflict.

As a manager, your job is decision-making and problem-solving. According to Sun Tzu, all problems in competition are opportunities in disguise. If there were no problems, there would be no opportunities for improvement. More to the point, ff there were no problems, organizations would not need managers to make decisions on a day-to-day basis.

However, you cannot be successful in competition simply by tackling every problem. You must tackle problems and make decisions that advance your position. As you advance your strategic position—and the position of your organization—you solve most problems by leaving them behind. The solution to most problems is identifying the weakness in your position that creates them and moving, advancing to a better position.

This perspective clarifies many competitive situations in a way that nothing else does. Sun Tzu's strategy insists that you make the most of your strengths to compensate for your weaknesses. Your strengths and weaknesses do not come from your situation alone, but from your relative position within the organization. To make the right decisions, you must understand the key elements that define your strategic position. Managers can easily use the ancient strategic principles of Sun Tzu's The Art of War to improve their performance as decision-makers.

The Art of War was written as a guide to overcoming obstacles. When we are faced with challenges, our natural reactions are "flight" or "fight," running away from a challenge or getting into conflict with people. As an alternative, Sun Tzu invented his science of competitive strategy. Strategy teaches us how to think about our strategic position and how we can advance it.

The Art of War offers a distinct, nonintuitive system for problem-solving. It solidifies a vague idea of a strategy into a clear, well-defined set of principles. Sun Tzu teaches that only a few key factors define your strategic position. Success goes not to the strongest or most aggressive but to those who best understand their situation and what their alternatives for improving it really are. When you have mastered Sun Tzu's system of strategy, you are able to almost instantly analyze competitive situations, spot opportunities, and make the appropriate decisions.

In our management adaptation, the basics of strategy are tailored to help you in your role as a decision-maker. Sun Tzu defined the world as consisting of two different environments. There are environments we control, where we can plan our actions, but there are also environments we cannot control—competitive environments where we must adapt to unexpected changes in the larger environment. In these situations, planning doesn't work. Instead, we must use strategic agility, movement based on a set of clear rules.

As we said earlier, this is translation of a certain set of ideas from a military context to the world of management. Since we have other specific adaptations of Sun Tzu's ideas for sales, marketing, career building, and running your own business, this work concentrates on the internal challenges of managing a team within a larger organization. These competitive challenges include dealing with employees, budgeting limited resources, managing time, improving procedures, and so on in competition with other managers. As a manager, you have to face a wide variety of issues, and we try to address a broad spectrum of them in this work.

As in all our *Art of War* adaptations, we present our management version side by side with our complete translation of the original text of *The Art of War*. We suggest that in reading this work, you read both texts and not just our management adaptation.

Sun Tzu wrote about the psychology of organizations. He wrote about the importance of innovation, momentum, and esprit de corps in competitive environments. Human organizations haven't changed in the last two thousand years and won't over the next two thousand. The only differences between modern organizations and the ancient military armies of Sun Tzu's era are the types of tools we use and the battlegrounds on which we compete.

Sun Tzu saw that, at their roots, all competitive challenges are economic. The secret to success, he concluded, is not just winning battles, but winning in a way that minimizes costs. This insight led to his entire approach to competition as an exercise in analysis, organization, positioning, momentum, and persuasion in an effort to minimize costly conflict. This same thinking will also be the basis for your success within your organization.

Though strategy shows you how to find success in competitive situations, Sun Tzu's recipe for success is to avoid unnecessary conflict. He sees such conflict as inherently costly. He teaches you how to handle direct, hostile confrontations when they cannot be avoided, but his basic approach is to defuse these situations before they occur. The approach is psychological: you must convince potential opponents to give you what you want without a fight. You must convince the people on your team to present a united front so that others will not challenge you.

Your goal as a manager shouldn't be just to get the work done but to get it done as efficiently as possible. All organizations compete for resources. Even as part of a larger organization, you will only continue to receive financial support if you are more productive than alternative providers of your service. The competitive environment gradually weeds out ineffective and inefficient organizational groups. Management is, in our era, the competition between groups of people for the most productive use of resources.

The military generals to whom Sun Tzu addressed his work were among the world's first serious managers. Like them, the leaders of today's organizations must compete with one another to survive.

Sun Tzu teaches that you must learn to think competitively. All organizations are in constant competition for customers and resources. Your customers, internal or external, always have alternatives to using your services. No matter how deeply your group is buried within the larger organization, you must know your competition and how you can best compete against it.

An essential ingredient of success is selecting the right focus for your activities. Every operation has limited resources. It is the manager's job to evaluate what must be done and what can be left undone, picking the best possible places to invest the organization's limited resources.

You must also continually innovate to improve your systems. Since operations are expensive, you must get projects done quickly and efficiently. According to the principles of classical strategy, standards and best practices must lead to innovation. Innovation then leads to new standards and best practices.

Sun Tzu wants you to pay close attention to the details of your environment. He enumerates various environmental factors, project stages, and organizational weaknesses and identifies ways to respond to them. These detailed lists are still surprisingly complete. Their advice is useful in analyzing any organizational situation. People are people. Organization is organization. Success is success.

According to Sun Tzu's teaching, managers cannot succeed through their own efforts alone. You don't create opportunities. You can defend your existing position from attack, but the competitive environment itself must provide the opportunities for organizational success. The secret is recognizing these opportunities when they present themselves, and, once you recognize them, you must have the confidence to act. Management sometimes requires watchful patience. At other times, management requires instant action. Sun Tzu feels that opportunities are always abundant, since every problem creates an opportunity, but that they are very difficult to recognize and act upon.

Sun Tzu sees success going to the best-informed and best-trained decision-makers. In Sun Tzu's system, there is no substitute for good information. He says outright that nothing is as important as acquiring good information. His ideas almost predicted today's information economy.

In general, the book is organized so that the broadest and longest-term issues, such as strategic analysis, are addressed in the initial chapters. Later chapters focus on the more specific approaches you must use to address specific situations. Despite its relatively short length, this book contains more valuable information about good management than other books two or three times its size.

Do not expect to appreciate all of its principles in one reading. As you face different types of challenges, you will discover different aspects of Sun Tzu's principles.

This books serves only as an introduction to Sun Tzu's methods. If you find these ideas interesting, we have developed a number of other works, both books, audios, and on-line courses for mastering these principles. Our most detailed work, the nine volumes of *Sun Tzu's Art of War Playbook,* breaks The Art of War down into a series of over 230 articles on the nine areas of strategic skill taught by Sun Tzu. To learn more, visit our site, SunTzus.com, the home of the Science of Strategy Institute.

Gary Gagliardi, 2014

♦ ♦ ♦

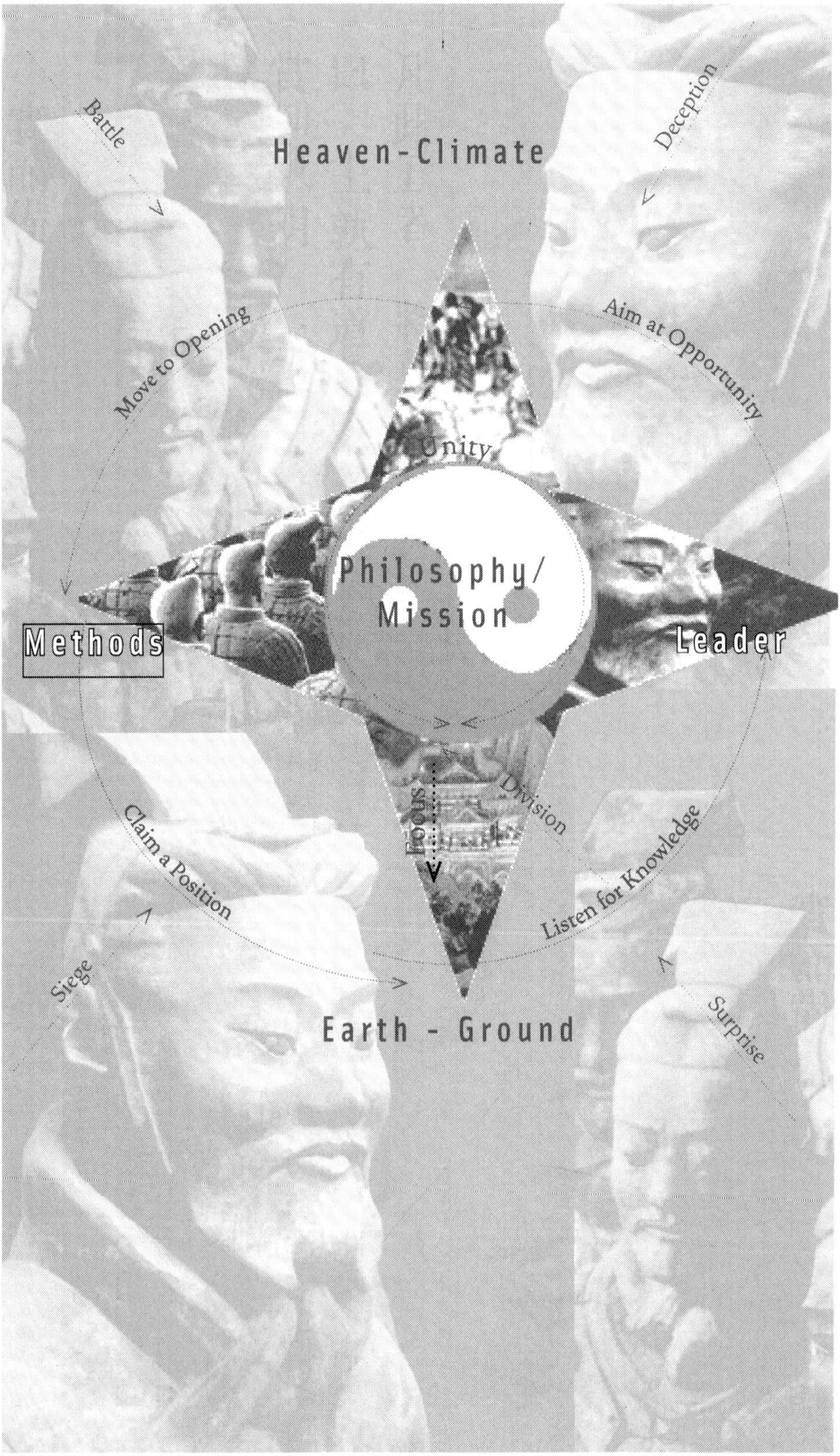

Heaven-Climate

Battle

Deception

Move to Opening

Aim at Opportunity

Unity

Philosophy/
Mission

Methods

Leader

Focus

Division

Claim a Position

Listen for Knowledge

Siege

Surprise

Earth - Ground

Introduction

Sun Tzu's Strategic System

This book is for managers who want to introduce themselves to the basic principles of Sun Tzu's competitive strategy and learn to apply them to making better competitive decisions. If you are new to Sun Tzu's strategic principles, you will find *The Art of War and The Art of Management* easier to understand if you first familiarize yourself with a few basic concepts, metaphors, and analogies. Sun Tzu's system is based on the traditions of Chinese science and philosophy and written from that perspective. Those traditions organized ideas around five elements (see facing page) that date back to the *I-Ching* and nine skills (see illustration above), derived from the Chinese *Bagua,* that symbolized eight directions of movement plus its center. This introduction gives you an overview of these key components of this strategic system.

Sun Tzu uses five elements to define all positions within a competitive environment. Understanding positions is the first skill that his strategic system teaches. These five elements—philosophy/mission, heaven/climate, earth/ground, the leader, and methods—provide the backbone of a strategic approach to management. All the other parts in his system—the nine skills, the four steps to advancing a position, the five faults of a leader, the six weaknesses of organizations, the six types of opportunities, the nine types of situations that arise in a campaign, and so on—flow from a good analysis of your relative position based on these five factors or elements.

The first element defining a position is called *philosophy* in the original text but it is better described in English as "the mission." A mission is the core of every position. It consists of the shared goals around which a team is built and the role your group exists to fulfill in the larger environment. Every department within an organization has its own mission, and the organization as a whole serves a larger mission. A clear idea of your mission within this larger purpose provides your group with its unity and focus.

Mission is the basis of two internal characteristics the Sun Tzu describes: *uniting* and *focusing* as creating competitive strength. Though these concepts are separate in English, in Chinese they are closely connected. In Sun Tzu's system, both arise directly from your shared goals or mission. *Uniting* holds the organization together. *Focusing* concentrates efforts in a single external goal. Teams lacking unity and focus from the element of mission are inherently weak..

The next two key elements define position within the larger environment. The importance of the environment is the great insight of Sun Tzu's work. He divides the environment into two opposite and yet complementary components, *heaven (climate)* and *ground (earth)*. Heaven and ground define the time and place of your position.

Heaven is the meaning of the Chinese character Sun Tzu used to describes time in terms of uncontrollable and unpredictable change. We usually use the term as "climate" in our training and "weather" in the English translation. The climate arises from trends that change over time. The cycle of the seasons are the most obvious trends in the natural environment, but every organization has its own business cycle and market climate. In today's business world, the pace of change based on increasing competition forces all organizations to improve in order to survive. This change erodes all existing positions and, at the same time, creates opportunities to advance your position.

Ground is the economic foundation on which your strategic position is based. It is both where you compete and what you compete for. Knowledge of the ground is the basis of all strategy. Within organizations, the shape of the ground is defined by a network of relationships, which can be very different from the formal organization chart. Unlike heaven, which is largely beyond our control, the ground that we control within the organization is determined by our own decisions. Choosing ground positions, moving to them, and utilizing them are the main basis of strategic method.

The *leader* is the next key factor in a strategic position. Decision-making is the unique responsibility of a leader in Sun Tzu's system. All managers are, by definition, leaders because they make decisions. Leadership is the realm of individual action and character. A manager masters strategy so that he or she can make the right decisions quickly.

Methods are the systems of the organization. Methods are, by definition, the realm of group action. A leader's decisions must utilize and build on existing systems to makes the organization's actions effective. A manager needs a deep understanding of all the systems in an organization that affect his or her mission.

Much of Sun Tzu's work is about "attack," by which he means not fighting others but moving into new areas to advance your position. Advancing your position is a matter of a *leader* making good decisions to develop your team's *methods* to take advantages of *climate* changes to secure better *ground.* to meet your *mission*. Though it is the basis for the entire work, Sun Tzu describes the basics of these five factors in the first few pages of his work.

Once you see your strategic position clearly in terms of these five factors, you advance your position. The balance of the book addresses specific methods for advancing a position. However, all this information can be boiled down to four simple steps. These steps are *listening for knowledge*, *aiming at opportunities*, *moving to openings*, and *claiming a position*. Every advance requires all four steps. If you miss a step, the process is more likely to create problems than to solve them.

Knowledge comes from understanding your ground, which requires *listening*. *Aim* means seeing how changing trends create an *opportunity* to advance. *Moving* means the ability to change methods to take advantage of an *opening*. *Claiming* means reaping the rewards from a new ground *position*.

Each of these four steps leads, naturally to the next in an endless cycle of advance. The more you learn about your ground, the more you need to identify new opportunities. Aiming at a new opportunity necessitates moving to new methods. Moving must give you a new position that you can claim. Claiming new ground creates new opportunities to listen and learn. Even if your attempted advance fails to yield profitable new ground, it cannot fail to generate new knowledge, which is the basis of the next cycle and your inevitable success.

Consciously or unconsciously, you go through this cycle every time you advance your position. When a decision is unsuccessful, it is simply because one of these four steps was not properly executed.

These four steps can be further broken down into a list of the eight strategic skills. Remember, Sun Tzu's first skill is understanding positions. Listening requires Sun Tzu's second key strategic skill of an outside developing perspective on your position and his third skill of using the change of climate for identifying opportunities. Aiming requires Sun Tzu's fourth and fifth skills, leveraging probability and minimizing mistakes. Moving requires his six and seventh skills of situation response and creating momentum.

Claiming requires his eighth and ninth skills of winning rewards and understanding vulnerabilities. All of these skills are covered in detail in our *Sun Tzu's Playbook*, which is divided into nine volumes, one for each skill. Articles from these nine volumes are referenced at the end of each chapter to connect the concepts presented in that chapter to the larger system.

The Art of War is a complete guide to executing these four steps in a wide variety of situations. However, much of it is written in a kind of code. These four steps are usually referenced in terms of metaphors. Listening for knowledge is referenced as sound. Thunder, music, and drums are all metaphors for listening. Aim is described as vision. Colors, lightning, and so on are all metaphors for foresight. Moving is marching. Claiming a position is variously described as gathering food, building, eating, digging in, and so on. We make all of these ideas easier to understand by adapting these metaphors into more easily understood management terms.

Just as these four steps are defined in terms of the five factors of a position, other strategic responses are defined in terms of these four steps. *Surprise* undermines knowledge. *Deception* confuses aim. *Battle*—which means meeting a challenge, not necessarily conflict—counters movement. *Siege* tries to overturn a position.

For a picture of Sun Tzu's system of five elements, four steps, and four responses, you can refer to the diagram that precedes this introduction.

If you find this introduction interesting, when you finish this book you may want to buy an overview of Sun Tzu's system written from a business perspective, *9 Formulas for Business Success: The Science of Strategy*. If you are looking for a more detailed analysis, you should explore the different volumes of *Sun Tzu's Art of War Playbook*, that provides a similar but much more extensive step-by-step guide to using Sun Tzu's system in business.

Chapter 1

Analysis: The Strategic Situation

As a manager, you need a framework for making decisions. In this first chapter, Sun Tzu provides a set of tools for evaluating your strategic position. The ideas presented here help you understand your potential within the organization and the challenges that you face in improving your position.

In the chapter's first section, Sun Tzu describes the five components that make up the basis for decision-making.

The second section describes the process of understanding your relative position by comparing it with the positions around you. What questions do you ask to evaluate your situation?

The third section addresses how you filter out critical elements from a flood of information.

In the fourth section, the problems of controlling and evaluating information in a competitive environment are discussed. Managers must control information to shape people's expectations, but they must also realize that the information they receive is also being managed.

Good management is often just a matter of doing the mathematics. In the chapter's final section, Sun Tzu discusses decision-making as a quantitative comparison: a balancing of pros and cons.

Your analysis of your situation provides the framework for the decisions you will make as a manager. In this first chapter, Sun Tzu provides an overview of the most basic rules for gathering and evaluating information.

Analysis

SUN TZU SAID:

This is war. 1
It is the most important skill in the nation.
It is the basis of life and death.
It is the philosophy of survival or destruction.
You must know it well.

6Your skill comes from five factors.
Study these factors when you plan war.
You must insist on knowing your situation.

1.	Discuss philosophy.
2.	Discuss the climate.
3.	Discuss the ground.
4.	Discuss leadership.
5.	Discuss military methods.

STRATEGY:

Strategy is the skill of advancing positions. Analyze your position by looking at five simple factors.

14It starts with your military philosophy.
Command your people in a way that gives
them a higher shared purpose.
You can lead them to death.
You can lead them to life.
They must never fear danger or dishonesty.

The Strategic Situation

THE MANAGEMENT WARRIOR HEARS:

1 This is management.
It is the skill that creates an organization.
It is the basis of start-ups and shutdowns.
It is the theory of endurance and elimination.
You can learn management.

Five elements determine your ability to manage.
Study these elements when you plan an organization.
You must understand:

1.   Management philosophy
2.   The use of time
3.   The contribution to value
4.   Leadership
5.   The decision-making process

MISSION:

Mission is the core of your position. A clear mission creates strength and focus within the organization.

Management begins with a philosophy.
When you manage people, you must give them a meaningful shared goal.
You can end their current jobs.
You can give them new work to do.
They must not feel threatened or used.

*Your position
exists within
a larger com-
petitive environ-
ment, which you
do not control.*

[19]Next, you have the climate.
It can be sunny or overcast.
It can be hot or cold.
It includes the timing of the seasons.

[23]Next is the terrain.
It can be distant or near.
It can be difficult or easy.
It can be open or narrow.
It also determines your life or death.

[28]Next is the commander.
He must be smart, trustworthy, caring, brave, and strict.

[30]Finally, you have your military methods.
They include the shape of your organization.
This comes from your management philosophy.
You must master their use.

[34]All five of these factors are critical.
As a commander, you must pay attention to them.
Understanding them brings victory.
Ignoring them means defeat.

DECISION:

*Good strategic
decisions are
based on ana-
lyzing how these
five factors
together create
your position.*

Next is the use of time.
Time can be tracked closely or disappear.
It can be productive or wasted.
You must understand the cycle of activities.

Next is everyone's contribution to value.
It can be eventual or immediate.
It can be arduous or effortless.
It can be broad or limited.
Creating value determines your organization's
existence.

Next is your leadership.
Develop everyone's foresight, self-reliance, and courage.

Finally, you have the decision-making process.
It determines how you build your organization.
Your management philosophy creates it.
You must master decision-making.

All five of these elements are necessary.
You must focus on them.
They will bring success.
Losing sight of them leads to failure.

AIM:

Your ability to foresee and leverage changes in the environment is the key to your organizational success.

TEAM:

Leaders need the teams to execute their decisions. Teams need leaders to make decisions so they can act.

You must learn through planning. 2
You must question the situation.

³You must ask:
Which government has the right philosophy?
Which commander has the skill?
Which season and place has the advantage?
Which method of command works?
Which group of forces has the strength?
Which officers and men have the training?
Which rewards and punishments make sense?
This tells when you will win and when you will lose.
Some commanders perform this analysis.
If you use these commanders, you will win.
Keep them.
Some commanders ignore this analysis.
If you use these commanders, you will lose.
Get rid of them.

Discover an opportunity by listening. 3
Adjust to the situation.
Get assistance from the outside.
Influence events.
Think about opportunities in terms of methods
you can control.

RELATIVITY:

No position is good or bad in itself. You only understand positions by comparing them to others.

2 You must educate yourself by analyzing.
You must understand your organization.

You must ask:
What is the right management philosophy?
Which managers are skillful?
Which uses of time and resources are valuable?
Which kind of management structure will work?
What are my organization's strengths?
Which managers and workers are trained?
What salaries and incentives make sense?
This is why some organizations work and others don't.
Some managers do this analysis.
If you employ them, you will be successful.
Keep them.
Too many managers never perform this analysis.
If you hire these managers, your organization will fail.
Get rid of them.

3 You find ways to advance simply by listening.
Look for what you need to change.
Find friends outside your organization.
Seek to make something happen.
Advance your position by making decisions that improve your systems.

LISTENING:

You must train your ears to become more sensitive to outside opinions that identify opportunities.

Warfare is one thing. 4
It is a philosophy of deception.

³When you are ready, you try to appear incapacitated.
When active, you pretend inactivity.
When you are close to the enemy, you appear distant.
When far away, you pretend you are near.

⁷You can have an advantage and still entice an opponent.
You can be disorganized and still be decisive.
You can be ready and still be preparing.
You can be strong and still avoid battle.
You can be angry and still stop yourself.
You can humble yourself and still be confident.
You can be playing and still be working.
You can be close to an ally and still part ways.
You can attack a place without planning to do so.
You can leave a place without giving away your plan.

¹⁷You will find a place where you can win.
You cannot first signal your intentions.

CONTROL:

Strategy is based on using the power of information. You control others by controlling their perceptions.

4 Remember that your situation is competitive.
Everyone find ways to control information.

When you are prepared, feign surprise.
When the department is busy, make light of the workload.
When problems are closing in, make them appear distant.
When deadlines are distant, make them appear imminent.

When you have everything under control, invite criticism.
When you are actually unprepared, avoid a sense of uncertainty.
When times are good, prepare for the bad.
Even if you can win political battles, you can still avoid them.
When you are angry, avoid making decisions.
You don't have to demonstrate your authority to maintain it.
Your people can have fun and still get work done.
You can be attached to an associate and not depend on him or her.
You can undertake challenges that you didn't plan on.
You can abandon bad ideas without letting others know.

You must find ways to excite and inspire people.
Never pass up an opportunity.

TESTING:

You can mislead others and they can mislead you. Successful managers continually test information.

Manage to avoid battle until your organization can count 5
on certain victory.
You must calculate many advantages.
Before you go to battle, your organization's analysis can indi-
cate that you may not win.
You can count few advantages.
Many advantages add up to victory.
Few advantages add up to defeat.
How can you know your advantages without analyzing them?
We can see where we are by means of our observations.
We can foresee our victory or defeat by planning.

♦ ♦ ♦

PATIENCE:

*Consciously
choosing not
to act is just as
important as
acting decisively
when the time is
right.*

Before accepting a management position, you must know that you can be successful.

You must see many opportunities.

Before making a management decision, avoid taking a position that is certain to fail.

You can see few opportunities.

Many opportunities add up to success.

Few opportunities add up to failure.

How can you understand the opportunities without analysis?

You must study the organization by observing it.

You can foresee success or failure by analysis.

✦ ✦ ✦

SUCCESS:

Success comes from focusing your limited resources on advancing along the path of least resistance.

Related Articles from *Sun Tzu's Playbook*

In this first chapter, Sun Tzu introduces the basics of positioning. We explore these ideas in more detail in our Sun Tzu's Art of War Playbook. *To learn the step-by-step techniques for positioning, we recommend the* Playbook *articles listed below.*

1.0.0 Strategic Positioning: developing relatively superior positions.

1.1.0 Position Paths: the continuity of strategic positions over time.

1.1.1 Position Dynamics: how all current positions evolve over time.

1.1.2 Defending Positions: defending current positions until new positions are established.

1.2 Subobjective Positions: the subjective and objective aspects of a position.

1.2.1 Competitive Landscapes: the arenas in which rivals jockey for position.

1.2.2 Exploiting Exploration: how competitive landscapes are searched and positions identified.

1.2.3 Position Complexity: how positions arise from interactions in complex environments.

1.3 Elemental Analysis: the relevant components of all competitive positions.

1.3.1 Competitive Comparison: competition as the comparison of positions.

1.3.2 Element Scalability: how elements of a position scale up to larger positions.

1.4 The External Environment: external conditions shaping strategic positions.

1.4.1 Climate Shift: forces of environmental change shaping temporary conditions.

1.4.2 Ground Features: the persistent resources that we can control.

1.5 Competing Agents: the key characteristics of competitors.

1.5.1 Command Leadership: individual decision-making.

1.5.2. Group Methods: systems for executing decisions.

1.6 Mission Values: the goals and values needed for motivation.

1.6.1 Shared Mission: finding goals that others can share.

1.6.2 Types of Motivations: hierarchies of motivation that define missions.

1.6.3 Shifting Priorities: how missions change according to temporary conditions.

Chapter 2

Going to War: Taking Control

For a manager, this chapter provides a great outline for understanding the consequences of management decisions. The focus is on simple economics. Sun Tzu focuses on the economics of strategy. He does not define victory as simply winning battles. He specifically defines success as making victory pay. This economic focus is one of the reasons that his strategy works so well in today's world.

How can management go wrong? Sun Tzu starts by discussing the debilitating cost of management in a competitive world and how easily money is wasted in this environment.

What are the costs and benefits of a given decision? The next short section describes the total cost and total reward of competition as unpredictable. Sun Tzu therefore advises minimizing spending to necessities.

Management requires communication and focus. In the third section, Sun Tzu covers the effect of distance on cost.

Everyone in the organization is responsible for generating value. The fourth section in this chapter offers a strategy for cost control: making every competitive venture pay for itself as directly and quickly as possible. Sun Tzu calls this "feeding off the enemy."

Your most important responsibilities as a leader are financial. In the chapter's final section, Sun Tzu argues that the ability to control costs is the key to a stable organization and that this depends on the knowledge of the leader.

Going to War

Sun Tzu said:

Everything depends on your use of military philosophy. 1
Moving the army requires thousands of vehicles.
These vehicles must be loaded thousands of times.
The army must carry a huge supply of arms.
You need ten thousand acres of grain.
This results in internal and external shortages.
Any army consumes resources like an invader.
It uses up glue and paint for wood.
It requires armor for its vehicles.
People complain about the waste of a vast
amount of metal.
It will set you back when you attempt to raise
tens of thousands of troops.

ECONOMY:

*Strategy teaches
that the key
to success is
making good
decisions about
using limited
resources.*

[12]Using a huge army makes war very expensive to win.
Long delays create a dull army and sharp
defeats.
Attacking enemy cities drains your forces.
Long violent campaigns that exhaust the
nation's resources are wrong.

Taking Control

THE MANAGEMENT WARRIOR HEARS:

1 Everything depends on your management philosophy.
Moving an organization requires thousands of decisions.
Your leadership is tested thousands of times.
People require equipment and supplies.
They need external customers to support them.
Some internal and external needs always go unmet.
Organizations always consume all their resources.
People require time and energy in management.
You must defend your decisions to move forward.
People always complain about how little they are paid.
The larger the organization you build, the more time you lose in managing it.

Growing an organization is costly and time consuming.
Delaying action dulls any organization and leads to failure.
Directly targeting entrenched opposition is costly.
Leadership decisions that deplete your organization's resources are wrong.

QUICKNESS:

Size and quickness are opposites. Both have their benefits, but quickness is always the most economical.

DARING:

*Going slowly
and "carefully"
is more costly
and dangerous
than moving
forward quickly.*

[16]Manage a dull army.
You will suffer sharp defeats.
You will drain your forces.
Your money will be used up.
Your rivals will multiply as your army col-
lapses and they will begin against you.
It doesn't matter how smart you are.
You cannot get ahead by taking losses!

[23]You hear of people going to war too quickly.
Still, you won't see a skilled war that lasts a
long time.

[25]You can fight a war for a long time or you can make your
nation strong.
You can't do both.

Make no assumptions about all the dangers in using **2**
military force.
Then you won't make assumptions about the benefits of
using arms either.

SPEED:

*Large is slow.
Small is fast. Do
not mistake an
accumulation of
costly resources
for power and
safety.*

[3]You want to make good use of war.
Do not raise troops repeatedly.
Do not carry too many supplies.
Choose to be useful to your nation.
Feed off the enemy.
Make your army carry only the provisions it
needs.

Let your organization get soft.

You will then suffer hard losses.

Expend your resources.

You thereby eliminate your options.

As an organization weakens, its employees lose confidence in the future.

It doesn't matter how smart you think you are.

You can't build an organization through failure.

MOMENTUM:

If you are not constantly making progress, change constantly erodes your existing position.

You can sometimes decide to act too quickly.

Still, the more you delay decisions, the more often you fail.

You can try to play it safe when you make decisions, or you can be successful.

You can't have it both ways.

2 You can never completely understand the consequences of any decision.

You can therefore never completely understand the potential in any decision either.

You must make the best use of your people.

Don't keep turning over your employees.

Find ways to minimize your expenditures.

Concentrate on creating value for others.

Contribute to success in the marketplace.

Give your people only what they need to create value.

CERTAINTY:

You cannot control what happens in the market, but you can control the way that you use resources.

The nation impoverishes itself shipping to troops that **3** are far away.

Distant transportation is costly for hundreds of families.

Buying goods with the army nearby is also expensive.

High prices also exhaust wealth.

If you exhaust your wealth, you then quickly hollow out your military.

Military forces consume a nation's wealth entirely.

War leaves households in the former heart of the nation with nothing.

[8]War destroys hundreds of families.

Out of every ten families, war leaves only seven.

War empties the government's storehouses.

Broken armies will get rid of their horses.

They will throw down their armor, helmets, and arrows.

They will lose their swords and shields.

They will leave their wagons without oxen.

War will consume 60 percent of everything you have.

Because of this, it is the intelligent **4** commander's duty to feed off the enemy.

ZERO SUM:

You must know the specific situations where your success has the benefit of hurting opponents.

[2]Use a cup of the enemy's food.

It is worth twenty of your own.

Win a bushel of the enemy's feed.

It is worth twenty of your own.

3 You cannot effectively lead an organization that is too spread out.

Coordination becomes too costly.

Using your internal resources exclusively is also expensive.

You must continually work to reduce costs.

Failure comes from exhausting your resources by supporting poor decisions.

Management decisions are what bankrupt a organization.

Poor management can destroy even the most successful organization.

Poor management destroys hundreds of companies.

Bad decision-making destroys organizations.

Poor organizational structure depletes limited resources.

Lack of resources forces you to abandon assets.

Your people will lose their faith and forget their abilities.

They will forget both production and maintenance.

The machinery of the organization will break down.

The organization's productivity depends on management.

4 Because of this, you must make sure that you run the organization profitably.

Take a dollar's worth of productivity today.

It is worth twenty dollars tomorrow.

Create a dollar's worth of customer value today.

It is worth twenty dollars of future potential.

RESULTS:

Competitive markets are unpredictable. Delaying immediate gains is seldom profitable over time.

⁶You can kill the enemy and frustrate him as well.
Take the enemy's strength from him by stealing away his money.

⁸Fight for the enemy's supply wagons.
Capture his supplies by using overwhelming force.
Reward the first who capture them.
Then change their banners and flags.
Mix them in with your own wagons to increase your supply line.
Keep your soldiers strong by providing for them.
This is what it means to beat the enemy while you grow more powerful.

Make victory in war pay for itself. **5**
Avoid expensive, long campaigns.
The military commander's knowledge is the key.
It determines whether the civilian officials can govern.
It determines whether the nation's households are peaceful or a danger to the state.

✦ ✦ ✦

MAKE IT PAY:

Success is defined only by its profitability.

You must support the organization and build confidence.

You need to create more value in the marketplace than you consume.

You compete for resources against all other organizations.

Find what is undervalued in the external market and buy it.

Reward those who find the right services and products.

Put your name and logo on these services and products.

Mix internal and external services and products to increase their value.

Retain your customers by being successful.

This is what it means to compete in the marketplace while growing more powerful.

5 Make success pay for itself.
Avoid long, expensive projects.

Your management decisions are the key.

They determine whether or not you can lead.

Your decisions determine whether your organization is productive or wasteful.

♦ ♦ ♦

CONTROL:

*Limit spending
to improve
your position.*

Related Articles from *Sun Tzu's Playbook*

In his second chapter, Sun Tzu teaches basic competitive economics. We explore these ideas in more detail in our **Sun Tzu's Art of War Playbook** *To learn the step-by-step techniques for economical political campaigning, we recommend the articles listed below.*

1.3.1 Competitive Comparison: competition as the comparison of positions.

1.6.1 Shared Mission: finding goals that others can share.

1.8.3 Cycle Time: speed in feedback and reaction.

1.8.4 Probabilistic Process: the role of chance in strategic processes and systems.

2.2.1 Personal Relationships: how information depends on personal relationships.

2.2.2 Mental Models: how mental models simplify decision-making.

2.3.4 Using Questions: using questions in gathering information and predicting reactions.

3.1 Strategic Economics: balancing the cost and benefits of positioning.

3.1.1 Resource Limitations: the inherent limitation of strategic resources.

3.1.2 Strategic Profitability: understanding gains and losses.

3.1.3 Conflict Cost: the costly nature of resolving competitive comparisons by conflict.

3.1.4 Openings: seeking openings to avoid costly conflict.

3.1.5 Unpredictable Value: the limitations of predicting the value of positions.

3.1.6 Time Limitations: the time limits on opportunities.

4.0 Leveraging Probability: better decisions regarding our choice of opportunities.

4.1 Future Potential: the limitations and potential of current and future positions.

4.2 Choosing Non-Action: choosing between action and non-action.

5.3 Reaction Time: the use of speed in choosing actions.

5.3.1 Speed and Quickness: the use of pace within a dynamic environment.

5.3.2 Opportunity Windows: the effect of speed upon opposition.

5.3.3 Information Freshness: choosing actions based on freshness of information.

5.4 Minimizing Action: minimizing waste, i.e., less is more.

5.4.1 Testing Value : choosing actions to test for value.

5.4.2 Successful Mistakes: learning from our mistakes.

5.5 Focused Power: size consideration in safe experimentation.

5.5.1 Force Size: limiting the size of force in an advance.

5.5.2 Distance Limitations: the use of short steps to reach distant goals.

Chapter 3

Planning an Attack: Preparing to Advance

The term "attack" doesn't mean fighting. It means moving into new territory. The central topic of this chapter is how you correctly prepare to expand your responsibilities.

Your first job is drawing your team together. In the chapter's first section, Sun Tzu says that unity and focus are required at every level of an organization. The goal of unity is not to win confrontations but to advance while avoiding confrontations.

You can improve your position only by taking action. The second section lists four approaches to advancing a position, the worst of which is directly challenging rivals.

You should not seek to make big advances all at once. In the third section, Sun Tzu suggests an incremental approach: addressing small, focused challenges where you are sure to be successful. He explains how the relative strength of your competitive position determines your basic tactics.

There is always the temptation to play internal politics, but you cannot advance your position by hurting your organization. The next section of text warns about the dangers of playing politics, putting your goals above those of the organization.

Decision-making depends on your knowledge. Sun Tzu details the five areas of knowledge that determine your ability to unite and concentrate your forces.

Sun Tzu ends by warning about the dangers of miscalculating the strength of your organization when facing competitive pressure.

Planning an Attack

SUN TZU SAID:

Everyone relies on the arts of war. 1
A united nation is strong.
A divided nation is weak.
A united army is strong.
A divided army is weak.
A united force is strong.
A divided force is weak.
United men are strong.
Divided men are weak.
A united unit is strong.
A divided unit is weak.

UNITY:

*Strategy teaches
that the size of
a team is not
nearly as im-
portant as how
united it is.*

[12]Unity works because it enables you to win
every battle you fight.
Still, this is the foolish goal of a weak leader.
Avoid battle and make the enemy's men surrender.
This is the right goal for a superior leader.

The best way to make war is to upset the enemy's plans. 2
The next best is to disrupt alliances.
The next best is to attack the opposing army.
The worst is to attack the enemy's cities.

Preparing to Advance

The management warrior hears:

1 Your organization must be competitive.
A united organization is successful.
A divided organization is unsuccessful.
A united department is effective.
A divided department is ineffective.
A united team is productive.
A divided team is wasteful.
Devoted employees are dependable.
Indifferent employees are undependable.
A united effort is solid.
A divided effort is fragile.

Focus:

Your ability to improve your position requires a clear focus on your priorities.

Unity works because it enables your organization
to address the challenges it faces.
This still doesn't make you a great manager.
Avoid challenges and accomplish your goals.
This is the right goal for a good manager.

2 The best way to advance is to do what is unexpected.
The next best is to win the support of your superiors.
The next best is to take over the responsibilities of others.
The worst is to attack the strengths of your rivals.

⁵This is what happens when you attack a city.
You can attempt it, but you can't finish it.
First you must make siege engines.
You need the right equipment and machinery.
It takes three months and still you cannot win.
Then you try to encircle the area.
You use three more months without making progress.
Your command still doesn't succeed and this angers you.
You then try to swarm the city.
This kills a third of your officers and men.
You are still unable to draw the enemy out of the city.
This attack is a disaster.

Make good use of war. 3
Make the enemy's troops surrender.
You can do this fighting only minor battles.
You can draw their men out of their cities.
You can do it with small attacks.
You can destroy the men of a nation.
You must keep your campaign short.

⁸You must be united in conflict from the top to the bottom.
Never stop when you are at war.
Your opportunity comes from being united.
In every situation, this is how your plan your attack as well.

This is what happens when you attack internal rivals.
You can easily start a battle, but you cannot end it.
First, you must build a case against your rival.
You need the right evidence and information.
This can take months and you won't be successful.
You then try to get others on your side.
After more months of effort, you still won't make progress.
You still cannot undermine your rival and this makes you impatient.
You then set up a showdown with your rival.
This undermines your credibility and effectiveness.
You are still unable to advance your position against the rival.
This approach is a disaster.

3 Make good use of your competitive skills.
You can win away support from your rival.
You can do this based on day-to-day performance.
You must lure rivals away from their strengths.
You do this gradually, a little at a time.
You can overcome any opposition.
You must keep your goals simple.

Good management joins the big picture with the smallest details.
Never stop your competitive positioning.
Your opportunities come from the big picture.
Use your situation to unite in the best way to advance your position.

¹²The rules for making war are:
If you outnumber enemy forces ten to one, surround them.
If you outnumber them five to one, attack them.
If you outnumber them two to one, divide them.
If you are equal, then find an advantageous battle.
If you are fewer, defend against them.
If you are much weaker, evade them.

¹⁹Small forces are not powerful.
However, large forces cannot catch them.

You must master command. 4
The nation must support you.

³Supporting the military makes the nation powerful.
Not supporting the military makes the nation weak.

⁵The army's position is made more difficult by politicians in
three different ways.
Ignorant of a military division's inability to advance, they
order an advance.
Ignorant of a military division's inability to withdraw, they
order a withdrawal.
We call this tying up the army.
They don't understands a military division's function.
Still, they think they can govern military divisions.
This confuses the army's officers.

The rules for overcoming internal opposition are:
If you have ten times the support, go around the opposition.
If you have five times the support, challenge the opposition.
If you have twice the support, divide the opposition.
If your support is equal, pick only battles you can easily win.
If your support is weaker, avoid confrontations.
If your support is much weaker, work quietly behind the scenes.

Small advances do not require much effort.
Major opposition cannot form against them.

4 You must make good decisions.
Your organization must support you.

Improving your organization strengthens your position.
Undermining your organization's focus weakens your position.

Playing internal politics can hurt your ability to advance in three different ways.
First, you can try to advance your position without understanding the limitations of your resources.
Second, you can try to get out of certain responsibilities without understanding their importance.
This can hamstring your position.
Third, if you play politics, you lose sight of the overall mission.
You will think only of what is best for your group.
This confuses your team's priorities.

[12]Politicians don't know the military division of authority.
They think all military divisions are the same.
This will create distrust among the army's officers.

[15]Military divisions can become confused and suspicious.
This invites invasion by many different rivals.
We say correctly that disorder in an army kills victory.

You must know five things to win: 5
Victory comes from knowing when to attack and when to avoid battle.
Victory comes from correctly using both large and small forces.
Victory comes from everyone sharing the same goals.
Victory comes from finding opportunities in problems.
Victory comes from having a capable commander and the government leaving him alone.
You must know these five things.
You then know the theory of victory.

We say: 6
"Know yourself and know your enemy.
You will be safe in every battle.
You may know yourself but not know the enemy.
You will then lose one battle for every one you win.
You may not know yourself or the enemy.
You will then lose every battle."

You must respect the responsibilities and decisions of others.
Do not expect everyone to have the same perspective.
If you do, other managers will never trust you..

Different departments can get caught up in internal politics.
This invites external competitors to steal the best people away.
Division within the organization kills its external success.

5 You must know five things to advance.
Success comes from knowing what needs doing and what does not.
Success comes from managing both large groups and small groups well.
Success comes from everyone sharing the same goals.
Success comes from turning problems into opportunities.
Success comes from putting the right people in place and letting them do their job.
You must learn these five things.
You then know the principles of success.

6 We say:
Know your supporters and your opponents.
You will be secure in every confrontation.
You can know your supporters but not your opponents.
Then, for every battle you win, you will lose another.
You may know neither your supporters nor your opponents.
You will then lose every battle.

Related Articles from *Sun Tzu's Playbook*

In this third chapter, Sun Tzu introduces the basics of advancing into new areas. To learn the step-by-step techniques involved, we recommend the Sun Tzu's Art of War Playbook articles listed below.

1.1.1 Position Dynamics: how all current positions are always getting better or worse.

1.1.2 Defending Positions: how we defend our current positions until new positions are established.

1.2 Subobjective Positions: the subjective and objective aspects of a position.

1.3.1 Competitive Comparison: competition as the comparison of positions.

1.7 Competitive Power: the sources of superiority in challenges.

1.7.1 Team Unity: strength by joining with others.

1.7.2 Goal Focus: strength as arising from concentrating efforts.

1.8 Progress Cycle: the adaptive loop by which positions are advanced.

1.8.1 Creation and Destruction: the creation and destruction of competitive positions.

1.8.2 The Adaptive Loop: the continual reiteration of position analysis.

2.3.6 Promises and Threats: the use of promises and threats as strategic moves.

2.4 Contact Networks: the range of contacts needed to create perspective.

2.4.1 Ground Perspective: getting information on a new competitive arena.

2.4.2 Climate Perspective: getting perspective on temporary external conditions.

3.0.0 Identifying Opportunities: the use of opportunities to advance a position.

3.1.3 Conflict Cost: the costly nature of resolving competitive comparisons by conflict.

3.2 Opportunity Creation: how change creates opportunities.

3.2.2 Opportunity Invisibility: why opportunities are always hidden.

3.2.4 Emptiness and Fullness: the transformations between strength and weakness.

3.4 Dis-Economies of Scale: how opportunities are created by the size of others.

3.4.2 Opportunity Fit: finding new opportunities that fit your size.

3.4.3 Reaction Lag: how size creates temporary openings.

3.5 Strength and Weakness: openings created by the strength of others.

3.6 Leveraging Subjectivity: openings between subjective and objective positions.

3.7 Defining the Ground: redefining a competitive arena to create relative mismatches.

5.6 Defensive Advances: balancing defending and advancing positions.

Chapter 4

Positioning: Advancing Solutions

Strategy provides a system for constantly improving your position rather than simply solving problems. While this chapter's lessons on positioning can be used in many ways, we have applied them specifically to advancing your department's or group's methods. Sun Tzu's concept of positioning means moving to a better position *only* when an opportunity presents itself.

Where does the opportunity for improvement come from? Sun Tzu starts by explaining that you can do no more than protect your existing position; only the larger competitive environment itself can create new opportunities for you.

Opportunities for innovation don't always exist. The second section explains that you must defend your current position while waiting for an opportunity for improvement to arise.

Management innovation depends upon execution. The third section of this chapter explains that execution requires two skills, moving in the right direction and making change easy.

How do you calculate whether or not an innovation is likely to work? Sun Tzu provides a simple formula for calculating whether or not you can succeed in winning a new position; this is done by calculating the relative balance of forces at the place and time of engagement.

Management is always about people. In the final section, Sun Tzu touches briefly on how critical positioning is in getting what you want out of the people with whom you work.

Positioning

Learn from the history of successful battles. 1
First, you should control the situation, not try to win.
If you adjust to the enemy, you will find a way to win.
The opportunity to win does not come from you.
The opportunity to win comes from your enemy.

⁶You must pick good battles.
You can control them until you can win.
You cannot win them until the enemy enables
your victory.

⁹We say:
You see the opportunity for victory; you don't
control it.

DEFENSE:

Strategy dictates that you must first make sure that your existing position is secure before moving to a new one.

Advancing Solutions

THE MANAGEMENT WARRIOR HEARS:

1 Learn from successful competitive thinking.
Your first actions should control your existing procedures.
If you adjust to change, you will see opportunities to improve them.
The opportunity for real improvement does not come from you.
Real opportunity comes from changing customer needs.

You must target the right challenges.
Avoid creating problems until an opportunity arises.
You cannot succeed by solving problems; you need an
opportunity to come along.

We say:
You must see the opportunity for achievement;
you cannot create it.

OPENINGS:

*You must take
advantage of the
opportunities
in your
environment
that situations
create for you.*

You are sometimes unable to win. 2
You must then defend.
You will eventually be able to win.
You must then attack.
Defend when you have insufficient strength.
Attack when you have a surplus of strength.

7You must defend yourself well.
Save your forces and dig in.
You must attack well.
Move your forces when you have a clear advantage.

11You must always protect yourself until you can completely
triumph.

Some may see how to win. 3
However, they cannot move their forces where they must.
This demonstrates limited ability.

4Some can struggle to a victory and the whole world may
praise their winning.
This also demonstrates a limited ability.

6Win as easily as picking up a fallen hair.
Don't use all of your forces.
See the time to move.
Don't try to find something clever.
Hear the clap of thunder.
Don't try to hear something subtle.

2 You cannot always find a way to shine in an organization.
You must then maintain your high standards.
You will eventually be in a position to demonstrate your skills.
Then you must commit to an advance.
Maintain standards when resources are stretched thin.
Improve systems when you have a surplus of resources.

You must maintain systems well.
Conserve your resources and control expenses.
You must innovate well.
Reorganize your operations when you have a clear opportunity.

You must always maintain existing systems until you have an
opportunity to really improve them.

3 Some managers have innovative ideas.
Yet they cannot assign resources to implement them.
This shows a limited ability.

Others struggle to solve a difficult problem, and everyone praises
their management skills.
This also shows a limited ability.

Innovation increases productivity effortlessly.
It doesn't exhaust your people.
Watch for the time to change.
Don't try to be too clever.
Listen for what makes a big difference.
Don't imagine subtle improvements that aren't there.

[12]Learn from the history of successful battles.
Victory goes to those who make winning easy.
A good battle is one that you will obviously win.
It doesn't take intelligence to win a reputation.
It doesn't take courage to achieve success.

[17]You must win your battles without effort.
Avoid difficult struggles.
Fight when your position must win.
You always win by preventing your defeat.

[21]You must engage only in winning battles.
Position yourself where you cannot lose.
Never waste an opportunity to defeat your enemy.

[24]You win a war by first assuring yourself of victory.
Only afterward do you look for a fight.
Outmaneuver the enemy before the first battle and then
fight to win.

BATTLE:

*In classical
strategy, battle
means meeting
an opponent's
challenge, not
necessarily get-
ting into a fight.*

Learn from the history of successful organizations.
Success goes to those who find an easier way.
A good idea is one that will obviously succeed.
You don't have to be a genius to achieve success.
You don't have to take risks to make an impact.

You want to improve your operations easily.
Avoid trying to fix intractable problems.
Fight for new approaches that put problems behind you.
You will always succeed if you avoid failure.

You must engage only in worthwhile improvements.
Move to methods that prevent problems.
Never pass up an opportunity to make a real contribution.

You implement successful solutions by first making sure they work.
Only then do you fight for their implementation.
Test new solutions before proposing that others accept them and
then you can fight for them.

SOLUTIONS:

*You cannot solve
every problem,
but you can put
most problems
behind you if
you advance
your methods.*

You must make good use of war. 4
Study military philosophy and the art of defense.
You can control your victory or defeat.

4This is the art of war:
"1.   Discuss the distances.
2.   Discuss your numbers.
3.   Discuss your calculations.
4.   Discuss your decisions.
5.   Discuss victory.

10The ground determines the distance.
The distance determines your numbers.
Your numbers determine your calculations.
Your calculations determine your decisions.
Your decisions determine your victory."

15Creating a winning war is like balancing a coin of gold
against a coin of silver.
Creating a losing war is like balancing a coin of silver
against a coin of gold.

Winning a battle is always a matter of people. 5
You pour them into battle like a flood of water pouring into
a deep gorge.
This is a matter of positioning.

4 You must use your management skills.
Study management philosophy and the basics of quality control.
You alone determine your success or failure.

This is the art of management:
1.   Talk about productivity.
2.   Talk about your statistics.
3.   Talk about your priorities.
4.   Talk about necessary changes.
5.   Talk about new goals.

The current systems determine your productivity.
Tracking productivity determines your statistics.
These statistics determine your priorities.
Your priorities determine the necessary changes.
These adjustments determine the new goals.

Creating a winning organization means insisting that something better replace what is good.
Organizational failure is a matter of accepting mediocrity in areas where excellence makes you more competitive.

5 Successful solutions always depend on people.
Changing practices and processes must carry workers forward into the future.
This is the secret of innovation.

♦ ♦ ♦

Related Articles from *Sun Tzu's Playbook*

In this fourth chapter, Sun Tzu explains the process for advancing positions. To learn the step-by-step techniques involved, we recommend the Sun Tzu's Art of War Playbook articles listed below.

1.1.2 Defending Positions: how we defend our current positions until new positions are established.

1.2 Subobjective Positions: the subjective and objective aspects of a position.

1.3.1 Competitive Comparison: competition as the comparison of positions.

1.7 Competitive Power: the sources of superiority in challenges.

1.8 Progress Cycle: the adaptive loop by which positions are advanced.

1.8.1 Creation and Destruction: the creation and destruction of competitive positions.

1.8.2 The Adaptive Loop: the continual reiteration of position analysis.

3.0.0 Identifying Opportunities: the use of opportunities to advance a position.

3.2 Opportunity Creation: how change creates opportunities.

Chapter 5

Momentum: Process Innovation

In the world of management, Sun Tzu's concept of momentum equates with the process of continual improvement: incrementally and continuously improving practices. The central topic of this chapter is creativity. By using creative approaches with standard practices, you create what Sun Tzu calls momentum.

Problem-solving requires using both standards and creativity. Sun Tzu begins by explaining that action can be either predictable or surprising.

Management isn't limited to enforcing standards or constant invention. The second section of this chapter explains that direct action and surprise depend on one another. Only by using them together can you create momentum, a stable environment of change. There are an infinite number of paths to innovation.

What role does timing play? Sun Tzu contrasts the ideas of momentum and timing. Momentum means building up pressures while timing releases it at the right time.

Progress in process innovation doesn't mean predictability. The fourth section addresses the chaotic nature of all competitive environments. Though you cannot eliminate this chaos, you can control it by planning your surprises or innovations at the right time.

But, as always, leadership requires managing people. In the final section, the pressure of momentum is explained in terms of its effect upon other people and their attitudes.

Momentum

Momentum requires developing a set of standards that others can depend upon.

SUN TZU SAID:

You control a large group the same as you control a few. 1
You just divide their ranks correctly.
You fight a large army the same as you fight a small one.
You only need the right position and communication.
You may meet a large enemy army.
You must be able to sustain an enemy attack without being defeated.
You must correctly use both surprise and direct action.
Your army's position must increase your strength.
Troops flanking an enemy can smash them like eggs.
You must correctly use both strength and weakness.

It is the same in all battles. 2
You use a direct approach to engage the enemy.
You use surprise to win.

4You must use surprise for a successful escape.
Surprise is as infinite as the weather and land.
Surprise is as inexhaustible as the flow of a river.

Process Innovation

INNOVATION:

THE MANAGEMENT WARRIOR HEARS:

Innovation of standards cre-ates a moving target that com-petitors cannot easily equal.

1 You manage a large organization the same as a small one.

You only need to distribute authority correctly.

You overcome major obstacles the same as small ones.

You must control the right process and train people to implement it.

You may encounter a huge roadblock.

You must be able to overcome serious difficulties without risking failure.

To do this, you must use both innovation and standards.

Real improvement is built on existing strengths.

Creative thinking can make problems disappear in an instant.

You must use both what you do well and what you can improve.

2 It is the same facing any challenge.

Doing what you know how to do well makes you competitive.

You must reinvent yourself to triumph.

You must use creativity when things inevitably go wrong.

Creativity is as endless as time and the environment.

Creativity is a never-ending river of human innovation.

7You can be stopped and yet recover the initiative.
You must use your days and months correctly.

9If you are defeated, you can recover.
You must use the four seasons correctly.

11There are only a few notes in the scale.
Yet you can always rearrange them.
You can never hear every song of victory.

14There are only a few basic colors.
Yet you can always mix them.
You can never see all the shades of victory.

17There are only a few flavors.
Yet you can always blend them.
You can never taste all the flavors of victory.

20You fight with momentum.
There are only a few types of surprises and direct actions.
Yet you can always vary the ones you use.
There is no limit to the ways you can win.

24Surprise and direct action give birth to each other.
They are like a circle without end.
You cannot exhaust all their possible combinations!

Surging water flows together rapidly. 3
Its pressure washes away boulders.
This is momentum.

Yesterday's failure becomes tomorrow's success.
You must get the most out of everyone's time.

You can encounter huge obstacles and still recover.
You must understand how everything changes over time.

There are only a few basic human actions.
Yet you can combine them any number of ways.
You can always find a better way to get the work done.

There are only a few basic steps in any process.
Yet you can mix them in unlimited ways.
You will never exhaust your ability to improve.

There are only a few different resources.
Yet you can always blend them.
You will never discover all the possible combinations.

You succeed with innovation.
You have a finite number of standards and potential improvements.
Yet you can continually adjust what you do.
There is no limit to the ways you can improve.

Innovative and standard methods need each other.
You must use both and move from one to the other.
Using both, you will never run out of good ideas.

3 Different technologies reinforce each other.
The new possibility of change washes away obstacles.
This is management innovation.

4A hawk suddenly strikes a bird.
Its contact alone kills the prey.
This is timing.

7You must fight only winning battles.
Your momentum must be overwhelming.
Your timing must be exact.

10Your momentum is like the tension of a bent crossbow.
Your timing is like the pulling of a trigger.

War is very complicated and confusing. 4
Battle is chaotic.
Nevertheless, you must not allow chaos.

4War is very sloppy and messy.
Positions turn around.
Nevertheless, you must never be defeated.

7Chaos gives birth to control.
Fear gives birth to courage.
Weakness gives birth to strength.

MOMENTUM:

Dependable standards and constant improvement create the pressure for people to change.

10You must control chaos.
This depends on your planning.
Your men must brave their fears.
This depends on their momentum.

14You have strengths and weaknesses.
These come from your position.

An innovation becomes suddenly practical.
It will sweep through the marketplace.
This is timing.

You must invest only in successful advances.
Your management innovation must be inspiring.
Your timing must be precise.

Your innovation creates pressure in the organization.
Your timing should release that pressure productively.

4 Customers are complicated and confused.
Industries are uncertain.
Your decisions must create dependability.

Processes are ineffective and inefficient.
New ideas outmode them.
This is why you must continuously improve.

Your customers' confusion demands your clarity.
People's uncertainty demands your confidence.
Your shortcomings create your opportunities.

You must organize what is disorganized.
This depends on your management analysis.
You must give your people confidence.
This depends on your use of innovation.

You have both good practices and weak ones.
There is no such thing as a perfect operation.

TIMING:

Good timing releases the pressure cre-ated by vision to give people a reason to make a change now.

[16]You must force the enemy to move to your advantage.
Use your position.
The enemy must follow you.
Surrender a position.
The enemy must take it.
You can offer an advantage to move him.
You can use your men to move him.
You can use your strength to hold him.

You want a successful battle. 5
To do this, you must seek momentum.
Do not just demand a good fight from your people.
You must pick good people and then give them momentum.

[5]You must create momentum.
You create it with your men during battle.
This is comparable to rolling trees and stones.
Trees and stones roll because of their shape and weight.
Offer men safety and they will stay calm.
Endanger them and they will act.
Give them a place and they will hold.
Round them up and they will march.

[13]You make your men powerful in battle with momentum.
This should be like rolling round stones down over a high,
steep cliff.
Momentum is critical.

You must put competitors at a disadvantage.

Use what you can control.

The industry must follow you.

Stop doing what is unnecessary.

Let others waste their time.

You must be competitive to motivate people.

You can use your people to motivate others.

You use your success to hold onto people.

5 You want to be successful.

You must use the power of innovation.

Do not just pressure your people to work harder.

Leverage good people by improving methods.

You must reinvent your business.

Your people must adjust to overcome difficulties.

Everyone should work together seamlessly.

People work together because of their skill and training.

Offer people job security and they will stay with you.

Make them see the common threat and they will act.

Give them standards that they can hold on to.

Give them incentives and they can change.

You make yourself powerful with innovation.

You can excite people's imagination so that doing the work becomes easy.

Use your innovation.

Related Articles from *Sun Tzu's Playbook*

In his fifth chapter, Sun Tzu explains the process for creating momentum. To learn the step-by-step techniques involved, we recommend the Sun Tzu's Art of War Playbook articles listed below.

1.2 Subobjective Positions: the subjective and objective aspects of a position.

7.0 Creating Momentum: how momentum requires creativity.

7.1 Order from Chaos: the value of chaos in creating competitive momentum.

7.1.1 Creating Surprise: creating surprise using our chaotic environment.

7.1.2 Momentum Psychology: the psychology of surprise.

7.1.3 Standards and Innovation: the methodology of creativity.

7.2 Standards First: the role of standards in creating connections with others.

7.2.1 Proven Methods: identifying and recognizing the limits of best practices.

7.2.2 Preparing Expectations: how we shape other people's expectations.

7.3 Strategic Innovation: a simple system for innovation.

7.3.1 Expected Elements: dividing processes and systems into components.

7.3.2 Elemental Rearrangement: seeing invention as rearranging proven elements.

7.3.3 Creative Innovation: the more advanced methods for innovation.

7.4 Competitive Timing: the role of timing in creating momentum.

7.4.1 Timing Methods: the three simplest methods of controlling timing.

7.4.2 Momentum Timing: the relative value of momentum at various times in a campaign.

7.4.3 Interrupting Patterns: how repetition creates patterns for surprise.

7.5 Momentum Limitations: the implications of momentum's temporary nature.

7.5.1 Momentum Conversion: converting momentum into positions with more value.

7.5.2 The Spread of Innovation: the spread of innovation to advance our position.

7.6 Productive Competition: using momentum to produce more resources.

7.6.1 Resource Discovery: using innovation to create value from seemingly worthless resources.

7.6.2 Ground Creation: the creation of new competitive ground to be successful.

Chapter 6

Weakness and Strength: Problems and Opportunities

Together the two concepts addressed in this chapter describe the mechanism by which you manage to avoid conflict and turn problems into opportunities. The two ideas discussed are both opposing and complementary concepts. You must accept that all strength comes from properly understanding your limitations.

How can managers avoid problems? Sun Tzu begins by offering methods by which we can keep the level of problems that we have to deal with under control.

Each problem is also an important opportunity for improvement. In the chapter's next section, Sun Tzu explains the need to use psychology in motivating people to change.

You have an opportunity to build teamwork in addressing problems. The third section discusses the way you prioritize improvement to reduce resistance. The fourth section addresses the need to control information and focus efforts. The fifth section shows you how to avoid creating opposition by keeping your plans a secret as long as possible.

Sometimes opposition is unavoidable. The sixth section addresses how you can keep opponents from undermining you.

For great managers, addressing problems as opportunities becomes a system. That is the focus of the seventh section.

In the final section, Sun Tzu explains how good strategy means following the path of least resistance.

Weakness and Strength

SUN TZU SAID:

Always arrive first to the empty battlefield to await the 1
enemy at your leisure.
After the battleground is occupied and you hurry to it,
fighting is more difficult.

3You want a successful battle.
Move your men, but not into opposing forces.

5You can make the enemy come to you.
Offer him an advantage.
You can make the enemy avoid coming to you.
Threaten him with danger.

WEAKNESS:

9When the enemy is fresh, you can tire him.
When he is well fed, you can starve him.
When he is relaxed, you can move him.

*Weaknesses
arise naturally
from needs that
arise over time.
Need also cre-
ates opportuni-
ties.*

Problems and Opportunities

THE MANAGEMENT WARRIOR HEARS:

1 If your operation keeps ahead of its workload, you can deal with problems when they arise.
If your operation is behind in its work, finding good solutions is nearly impossible.

You want a successful operation.
Reorganize your systems but do not create more work.

You can encourage the creation of problems.
Offer people incentives to take shortcuts.
You can discourage the creation of problems.
Penalize those who do sloppy work.

If your people are too comfortable, challenge them.
If your people are satisfied, increase their desires.
If your people are lethargic, get them moving.

STRENGTHS:

All managers have areas of strength that make some tasks easier for them than for other people.

Leave any place without haste. 2
Hurry to where you are unexpected.
You can easily march hundreds of miles without tiring.
To do so, travel through areas that are
deserted.

AVOIDANCE:

Success depends upon avoid-ing operational challenges while you move to develop better positions.

You must take whatever you attack.
Attack when there is no defense.
You must have walls to defend.
Defend where it is impossible to attack.

9Be skilled in attacking.
Give the enemy no idea where to defend.

11Be skillful in your defense.
Give the enemy no idea where to attack.

Be subtle! Be subtle! 3
Arrive without any clear formation.
Ghostly! Ghostly!
Arrive without a sound.
You must use all your skill to control the enemy's decisions.

6Advance quietly and he can't defend.
Charge through his openings.
Withdraw quietly and he cannot chase you.
Move quickly so that he cannot catch you.

2 Change established procedures and roles gradually.

Quickly implement unexpected new responsibilities.

You can get a lot of work done without making people work hard.

To do so, you must avoid obstacles to getting the work done.

You must cement the changes you make.

Make changes where there is no opposition.

You must establish processes that will last.

Make it impossible to return to old habits.

Be skilled in changing what doesn't work.

Work in areas where no one has a stake to defend.

CHANGE:

Avoid opposition in making gradual improvements and cement those improvements in place.

Be skillful in protecting what does work.

Create measurements that show it is working.

3 You must make changes subtly.

Don't let potential opposition know what you plan.

You must keep quiet.

Make decisions without a fuss.

You must be skilled in controlling people's perceptions.

If you keep your decisions quiet, others can't oppose you.

Look for your openings.

If you quietly end low-value services, no one will complain.

Move quickly so that opposition cannot form.

[10]Always pick your own battles.
The enemy can hide behind high walls and deep trenches.
Do not try to win by fighting him directly.
Instead, attack a place that he must recapture.
Avoid the battles that you don't want.
You can divide the ground and yet defend it.
Don't give the enemy anything to win.
Divert him by coming to where you defend.

Make other men take a position while you take none. **4**
Then focus your forces where the enemy divides his forces.
Where you focus, you unite your forces.
When the enemy divides, he creates many small groups.
You want your large group to attack one of his small ones.
Then you have many men where the enemy has but a few.
Your larger force can overwhelm his smaller one.
Then go on to the next small enemy group.
You can take them one at a time.

You must keep the place that you have chosen as a **5**
battleground a secret.
The enemy must not know.
Force the enemy to prepare his defense in
many places.
You want the enemy to defend many places.
Then you can choose where to fight.
His forces will be weak there.

SECRECY:

*You cannot
exploit the
weakness of
other people if
everyone knows
what you are
doing.*

You must always prioritize your challenges.

Some problems are systemic.

You can't overcome them by attacking them directly.

Instead, find a new approach that turns them around.

Avoid confrontations that you cannot win.

You can divide the work and defend its reassignment.

Don't leave potential opposition anything to attack.

Distract opponents to keep them from seeing what you are up to.

4 Identify where the challenge lies before you make a move.

Focus on the weak places in your processes.

When you link responsibilities, you unite your people.

Blame divides people and creates small groups.

The pressure toward unity must outweigh divisiveness.

Focus on teamwork rather than the self-interest of the few.

A united team can sweep away small cliques.

After tackling one problem, go on to the next.

Tackle problems one at a time.

5 You must keep any big changes that you are planning a secret until you are ready to make them.

Keep potential opponents in the dark.

Bring up many possible problems and potential solutions.

Force people to justify every time-consuming task.

You can then choose where you want to focus.

Eliminate tasks that are hard to justify.

STRENGTH:

Strength does not come from size or status. It comes from targeting efforts on overcoming weaknesses.

7If he reinforces his front lines, he depletes his rear.
If he reinforces his rear, he depletes his front.
If he reinforces his right flank, he depletes his left.
If he reinforces his left flank, he depletes his right.
Without knowing the place of attack, he cannot prepare.
Without knowing the right place, he will be weak everywhere.

WEAK POINTS:

You must see a opponent's most serious weak points and focus your strengths on exploiting them.

13The enemy has weak points.
Prepare your men against them.
He has strong points.
Make his men prepare themselves against you.

You must know the battleground. 6
You must know the time of battle.
You can then travel a thousand miles and
still win the battle.

4The enemy should not know the battle-
ground.
He shouldn't know the time of battle.
His left flank will be unable to support his right.
His right will be unable to support his left.
His front lines will be unable to support his rear.
His rear will be unable to support his front.
His support is distant even if it is only ten miles away.
What unknown place can be close?

12You control the balance of forces.
The enemy may have many men but they are superfluous.
How can they help him to victory?

If opposition builds in one area, it lessens in another.
If people want one thing, they must sacrifice something else.
If they are adamant on some issues, they loosen up on others.
If some things are important, people compromise elsewhere.
Not knowing your intentions, opposition cannot form.
Incite opposition elsewhere so you can move where needed.

All organizations have weaknesses.
You must prepare to minimize them.
All organizations have opportunities.
Make your people focus on leveraging them.

NEEDS:

Every organization has an infinite number of needs. You must choose those that you can best address.

6 You must know exactly what your goals are.
You must time your decisions precisely.
No matter how difficult the situation, you can still succeed.

Potential opponents must not know the changes you plan.
They must never know the time you plan to move.
Opposition on different issues must not unite.
General opposition must not focus on one issue.
Productivity must not disguise weaknesses.
Weaknesses must not stop productivity.
People won't oppose changes that they don't expect.
How can unknown plans be opposed?

You decide the balance of emotion.
People may vaguely oppose doing what is needed.
How can they stop you from succeeding?

[15]We say:
You must let victory happen.

[17]The enemy may have many men.
You can still control him without a fight.

When you form your strategy, know the strengths and 7
weaknesses of your plan.
When you execute a plan, know how to manage both action
and inaction.
When you take a position, know the deadly and the winning
grounds.
When you enter into battle, know when you have too many
or too few men.

[5]Use your position as your war's centerpiece.
Arrive at the battle without a formation.
Don't take a position in advance.
Then even the best spies can't report it.
Even the wisest general cannot plan to counter you.
Take a position where you can triumph using superior numbers.
Keep opposing forces ignorant.
Everyone should learn your location after your position has
given you success.
No one should know how your location gives you a winning
position.
Make a successful battle one from which the enemy cannot
recover.
You must continually adjust your position to his position.

This is always true.

You must allow yourself to succeed.

Your problems may be overwhelming.

You can still solve them by avoiding confrontations.

7 When you plan your strategy, know the strengths and weaknesses of your analysis.

When you execute your plan, know what needs to be done and what can be left undone.

When you make a decision, know exactly what will work and what will not.

When you move, know when you have too many or too few resources.

Use your credibility as leverage for your projects.

Go into every situation with an open mind.

Avoid being easily predictable.

Then the opposition can't spread rumors against you.

Even the most adamant opponent cannot counter you.

Make decisions that have the weight of the organization behind them.

Keep potential opposition in the dark.

Potential opponents should learn about your project only after it succeeds.

They should not see how you were able to create the support that you needed.

Make your success so clear-cut that others cannot disparage or minimize it.

Always adjust your plan to weaken any opposition.

Manage your military position like water. 8
Water takes every shape.
It avoids the high and moves to the low.
Your war can take any shape.
It must avoid the strong and strike the weak.
Water follows the shape of the land that directs its flow.
Your forces follow the enemy, who determines how you win.

[8]Make war without a standard approach.
Water has no consistent shape.
If you follow the enemy's shifts and changes, you can always
find a way to win.
We call this shadowing.

[12]Fight five different campaigns without a firm rule for victory.
Use all four seasons without a consistent position.
Your timing must be sudden.
A few weeks determine your failure or success.

ADJUSTMENT:

*Continuously
adjust to con-
tinuous change.*

8 You must remain flexible in your decision-making.
Decisions can take any shape.
Avoid what is difficult and do what comes easily.
Your organization can take any form.
You must leverage opportunities and minimize problems.
Follow the shifts in situations in order to direct their course.
The organization's skills overcome problems to find success.

You must avoid rigid plans and procedures.
Ideas have no consistent shape.
By following the shifts and changes in the situation, you can always succeed.
This is called opportunism.

Use new ideas; no standard approach is always successful.
Use every moment to invent new approaches.
You must make decisions quickly.
An instant can determine your success or failure.

Urgency:

Managers must make decisions quickly.

Related Articles from *Sun Tzu's Playbook*

In chapter six, Sun Tzu explains how to find opportunities by leveraging opposites. To learn the step-by-step techniques involved, we recommend the Sun Tzu's Art of War Playbook *articles listed below.*

1.2.1 Competitive Landscapes: the arenas in which rivals jockey for position.

1.2.2 Exploiting Exploration: how competitive landscapes are searched and positions utilized.

1.2.3 Position Complexity: how strategic positions arise from interactions in complex environments.

1.3.1 Competitive Comparison: competition as the comparison of positions.

2.4 Contact Networks: the range of contacts needed to create perspective.

2.4.1 Ground Perspective: getting information on a new competitive arena.

2.4.2 Climate Perspective: getting perspective on temporary external conditions.

2.4.3 Command Perspective: developing sources for understanding decision-makers.

2.4.4 Methods Perspective: developing contacts who understand best practices.

2.4.5 Mission Perspective: how we develop and use a perspective on motivation.

2.5 The Big Picture: building big-picture strategic awareness.

2.6 Knowledge Leverage: getting competitive value out of knowledge.

2.7 Information Secrecy: the role of limiting information in controlling relationships.

3.2.3 Complementary Opposites: the dynamics of balance from opposing forces.

Chapter 7

Armed Conflict: Internal Politics

For you as a manager, this chapter serves to focus your efforts on making your organization more competitive by avoiding internal politics. In this chapter, Sun Tzu warns against engaging in direct confrontations that do not create a real opportunity. The latter part of the chapter covers techniques for succeeding in such internal political battles when they occur.

For a manager, getting caught up in organizational politics is dangerous. Sun Tzu begins by explaining the dangers of such battles and that they cannot be undertaken accidentally.

How can you hurt your internal political opponents? Section two explains the disasters that occur when you rush into battle with such opponents just to damage them.

You need to have a good image in the organization. The third section reemphasizes the need for deception—that is, controlling others' perceptions—when confrontations are unavoidable.

If you don't publicize your successes, who will? In section four here, Sun Tzu discusses the need for good methods of communication in political situations. Good communication is the primary key to winning all such battles.

There is a psychology to confrontation. The fifth section addresses the proper timing for unavoidable confrontations.

To summarize his rules of fighting internal battles, in the final section Sun Tzu provides a short but critical list of rules for avoiding mistakes during confrontations with opponents.

Armed Conflict

Everyone uses the arts of war. 1
You accept orders from the government.
Then you assemble your army.
You organize your men and build camps.
You must avoid disasters from armed conflict.

⁶Seeking armed conflict can be disastrous.
Because of this, a detour can be the shortest path.
Because of this, problems can become
opportunities.

⁹Use an indirect route as your highway.
Use the search for advantage to guide you.
When you fall behind, you must catch up.
When you get ahead, you must wait.
You must know the detour that most directly
accomplishes your plan.

¹⁴Undertake armed conflict when it creates an
advantage.
Seeking armed conflict for its own sake is
dangerous.

CONFLICT:

*Strategy teaches
that conflict is
always costly
so it is ideally
avoided when-
ever possible.*

Internal Politics

THE MANAGEMENT WARRIOR HEARS:

1 Everyone uses the art of management.
You get your mission from upper management.
Then you build your department.
You must hire the right people and budget resources.
You must always avoid mistakes in handling internal politics.

Ignoring the reality of internal politics is disastrous.
Because of this, you must find new approaches.
You must look for ways to make opponents into supporters.

You must do what is unexpected to make progress.
Let the opportunities you find guide your progress.
Don't get out of step with the organization.
You don't want to be too far ahead or behind.
You must find a way to make everyone look good while meeting your goals.

DETOUR:

Leverage internal politics when it creates real opportunities.
Seeking political confrontations just to win them is deadly.

The quickest way to get what you want is to go out of your way to give other people what they want.

You can build up an army to fight for an advantage. 2
Then you won't catch the enemy.
You can force your army to go fight for an advantage.
Then you abandon your heavy supply wagons.

5You keep only your armor and hurry after the enemy.
You avoid stopping day or night.
You use many roads at the same time.
You go hundreds of miles to fight for an advantage.
Then the enemy catches your commanders and your army.
Your strong soldiers get there first.
Your weaker soldiers follow behind.
Using this approach, only one in ten will arrive.
You can try to go fifty miles to fight for an advantage.
Then your commanders and army will stumble.
Using this method, only half of your soldiers will make it.
You can try to go thirty miles to fight for an advantage.
Then only two out of three will get there.

18If you make your army travel without good
supply lines, your army will die.
Without supplies and food, your army will die.
If you don't save the harvest, your army will
die.

FIGHTING:

You do not create opportunities by fighting for them. The use of force without leverage is wasted effort.

2 You can devote your resources to fighting for recognition.
Then your opponents will make you look foolish.
You can get caught up with the idea of winning internal battles.
You then lose your broader support in the organization.

You can try to protect yourself by showing up your rivals.
You can work day and night.
You can try to do more than you can do.
You can go out of your way looking for ways to embarrass them.
Then your rivals will strike back, finding a way to discredit you.
Your successes are forgotten.
Your motives are what the organization sees.
Only a small fraction of your efforts will be rewarded.
You can try to outshine opponents in less dramatic ways.
You will still eventually make a mistake.
You will be only half as successful as you could be.
You cannot go out of your way to attack opponents.
It will cost you more than it is worth.

If you try to make progress in the organization
without broad support, you will fail.
Without focusing your time and effort, you fail.
If you do not concentrate on your responsibilities, you will fail.

RIVALS:

*You must know
what internal
rivals are doing,
but you cannot
succeed if you
focus just on
stopping them.*

²¹Do not let any of your potential enemies know what you are planning.
Still, you must not hesitate to form alliances.
You must know the mountains and forests.
You must know where the obstructions are.
You must know where the marshes are.
If you don't, you cannot move the army.
If you don't, you must use local guides.
If you don't, you can't take advantage of the terrain.

You make war by making a false stand. 3
By finding an advantage, you can move.
By dividing and joining, you can reinvent yourself and transform the situation.
You can move as quickly as the wind.
You can rise like the forest.
You can invade and plunder like fire.
You can stay as motionless as a mountain.
You can be as mysterious as the fog.
You can strike like sounding thunder.

DECEPTION:

Success comes from controlling people's perceptions by shaping the way situations must appear to them.

¹⁰Divide your troops to plunder the villages.
When on open ground, dividing is an advantage.
Don't worry about organization; just move.
Be the first to find a new route that leads directly to a winning plan.
This is how you are successful at armed conflict.

Instead, you must keep political opponents from knowing that you see them as rivals.

Always, you must look for organizational allies.

Cultivate relationships with those above and around you.

You must know where your potential roadblocks are.

You must know where you might get bogged down.

If you don't, you can't improve your political position.

You must develop information sources.

If you don't, you won't hear about opportunities to shine.

3 You must control appearances to succeed in your goals.

Look for opportunities to improve your political standing.

By splitting alliances and joining alliances, you can reinvent your role and transform your position.

You must make progress quickly when the trends are right.

You can rise slowly over time.

You can generate excitement and appear hot.

You can avoid unwanted attention and appear solid.

You can keep quiet about your intentions.

You can make a lot of noise to get noticed.

Divide your resources to pursue opportunities.

When you are unopposed, spreading yourself thin can work.

Worry less about plans; make things happen.

Try new things and be the first to create a break-through success for your organization.

This is how you are successful in developing power.

OPPORTUNISM:

When your focus on making friends rather than fighting enemies, you can find more opportunities.

Military experience says: 4
"You can speak, but you will not be heard.
You must use gongs and drums.
You cannot really see your forces just by looking.
You must use banners and flags."

6You must master gongs, drums, banners, and flags.
Place people as a single unit where they can all see and hear.
You must unite them as one.
Then the brave cannot advance alone.
The fearful cannot withdraw alone.
You must force them to act as a group.

12In night battles, you must use numerous fires and drums.
In day battles, you must use many banners and flags.
You must position your people to control what they see and hear.

You control your army by controlling its morale. 5
As a general, you must be able to control emotions.

3In the morning, a person's energy is high.
During the day, it fades.
By evening, a person's thoughts turn to home.
You must use your troops wisely.
Avoid the enemy's high spirits.
Strike when his men are lazy and want to go home.
This is how you master energy.

4 Management experience teaches us this:
"You can be successful, but your success will be overlooked.
You must promote your success to get noticed.
Superiors cannot know your capabilities just by looking.
You must make your success interesting."

Use reporting and novelty to get upper management's attention.
Make sure that your successes are generally known.
Use your success to bring the team together.
Do not let the most aggressive take credit alone.
Give credit to everyone involved.
You want your department to work together.

If you are unknown in the organization, you must advertise more.
If you are better known, you must still win attention.
You must consider what people at every level of the organization
see and hear about you.

5 You control your people by considering people's feelings.
As a manager, you must control your own emotions.

In the morning, people are busy.
During the day, their energy fades.
In the evening, people want to go home.
You must time your contacts wisely.
Avoid bothering people when they are busy.
Get their agreement when they want to go home.
This is how you make agreement easy.

¹⁰Use discipline to await the chaos of battle.
Keep relaxed to await a crisis.
This is how you master emotion.

¹³Stay close to home to await a distant enemy.
Stay comfortable to await the weary enemy.
Stay well fed to await the hungry enemy.
This is how you master power.

Don't entice the enemy when his ranks are orderly. 6
You must not attack when his formations are solid.
This is how you master adaptation.

⁴You must follow these military rules.
Do not take a position facing the high ground.
Do not oppose those with their backs to the wall.
Do not follow those who pretend to flee.
Do not attack the enemy's strongest men.
Do not swallow the enemy's bait.
Do not block an army that is heading home.
Leave an escape outlet for a surrounded army.
Do not press a desperate foe.
This is how you use military skills.

EMOTION:

*Strategy teaches
that emotion is
the key to ac-
tion. If you con-
trol emotions,
you control
actions.*

When internal problems arise, don't overreact.
Keep calm in every crisis.
This is how you master your own emotions.

Stay close to your duties, and political enemies will be frustrated.
Stay well prepared and wear down your critics.
Stay within budget and don't give your critics ammunition.
This is how you master power.

6 Do not antagonize opponents when they are well prepared.
You must avoid conflicts with rivals who are well connected.
This is how you master flexibility.

You must follow these rules in your management:
Do not take a position opposing upper management.
Do not offer criticism without offering alternatives.
Do not follow those who have failed in the past.
Do not attack your opponent's successes.
Do not believe everything you hear.
Do not create problems for those finishing a job.
Leave everyone a way to save face.
Do not create unhappy coworkers.
This is the art of management.

◆ ◆ ◆

GREATNESS:

Your message must not be how great you are, but how you can make the organization great.

Related Articles from *Sun Tzu's Playbook*

In chapter seven, Sun Tzu teaches us to focus on building positions instead of on tearing down opponents. To learn the step-by-step techniques involved, we recommend the Sun Tzu's Art of War Playbook *articles listed below.*

1.2.1 Competitive Landscapes: the arenas in which rivals jockey for position.

1.3.1 Competitive Comparison: competition as the comparison of positions.

1.5 Competing Agents: characteristics of competitors.

1.7 Competitive Power: the sources of superiority in challenges.

1.8.1 Creation and Destruction: the creation and destruction of competitive positions.

1.9 Competition and Production: the two opposing skill sets of competition and production.

2.1.3 Strategic Deception: misinformation and disinformation in competition.

2.6 Knowledge Leverage: getting competitive value out of knowledge.

2.7 Information Secrecy: the role of secrecy in relationships.

3.1 Strategic Economics: balancing the cost and benefits of positioning.

3.1.1 Resource Limitations: the inherent limitation of strategic resources.

3.1.3 Conflict Cost: the costly nature of resolving competitive comparisons by conflict.

3.1.6 Time Limitations: understanding the time limits on opportunities.

3.7 Defining the Ground: redefining a competitive arena to create relative mismatches.

4.7 Competitive Weakness: how certain opportunities can bring out our weaknesses.

6.1.2 Prioritizing Conditions: parsing complex competitive conditions into simple responses.

6.8 Competitive Psychology: improving competitive psychology even in adversity and failure.

7.4 Competitive Timing: the role of timing in creating momentum.

7.6 Productive Competition: using momentum to produce more resources.

7.6.2 Ground Creation: the creation of new competitive ground to be successful.

8.5 Leveraging Emotions: how we use emotion to obtain rewards.

9.5.2 Avoiding Emotion: the danger of exploiting environmental vulnerabilities for purely emotion reasons.

Chapter 8

Adaptability: Continuous Improvement

In management, you must constantly improve your organization to meet your customers' changing needs. The topic of this chapter is the need to continually change your plans based upon changing conditions. In Sun Tzu's view, successful strategies must be dynamic and be based on a willingness to change.

As the pace of change quickens, managers must build change into their operations. In the chapter's first section, Sun Tzu lists situations (covered in greater detail in several other chapters) that demonstrate the need to constantly change your plans.

Your viewpoint must also change. The next short section makes the point that you can be creative and constantly adapt your methods without being inconsistent in your results.

The best defense is a good offense. The third section, also short, explains that you can use the dynamics of competitive situations to control your opponents' behavior.

All managers have to be prepared to meet unexpected problems. Sun Tzu covers the need to address the unpredictability of opponents in planning the defense of your position.

What are your weaknesses as a manager? In the final section, Sun Tzu lists the five weaknesses of leaders and explains how easily these weaknesses can be exploited in the dynamics of competition.

Adaptability

SUN TZU SAID:

Everyone uses the arts of war. 1
As a general, you get your orders from the government.
You gather your troops.
On dangerous ground, you must not camp.
Where the roads intersect, you must join your allies.
When an area is cut off, you must not delay in it.
When you are surrounded, you must scheme.
In a life-or-death situation, you must fight.
There are roads that you must not take.
There are armies that you must not fight.
There are strongholds that you must not attack.
There are positions that you must not defend.
There are government commands that must
not be obeyed.

ADAPTABILITY:

Adaptability doesn't mean doing what you want. It means knowing the appropriate response to the situation.

[14]Military leaders must be experts in knowing
how to adapt to find an advantage.
This will teach you the use of war.

Continuous Improvement

THE MANAGEMENT WARRIOR HEARS:

1 Everyone uses management skills.
You get your orders from the management hierarchy.
You organize your people.
When you run into problems, you keep going.
Where interests intersect, you find partners.
When a situation leads nowhere, you get out of it.
When problems surround you, you need new ideas.
When you are in a do-or-die situation, you must fight.
There are paths that you must avoid.
There are powers that you don't want to oppose.
There are responsibilities that you do not want.
There are positions that you cannot defend.
There are directions from upper management that
you must ignore.

RESILIENCE:

Great managers must be geniuses at knowing how
to adapt to succeed.
This will teach you the use of management.

*You become
more resilient
when you see
that no situation
is good or bad
in itself. All that
matters is your
response.*

[16]Some commanders are not open to making adjustments to
find an advantage.
They can know the shape of the terrain.
Still, they cannot find an advantageous position.

[19]Some military commanders do not know how to adjust
their methods.
They can find an advantageous position.
Still, they cannot use their men effectively.

You must be creative in your planning. 2
You must adapt to your opportunities and weaknesses.
You can use a variety of approaches and still have a
consistent result.
You must adjust to a variety of problems and consistently
solve them.

You can deter your potential enemy by using his 3
weaknesses against him.
You can keep your potential enemy's army busy by giving it
work to do.

PLANNING:

You can rush your potential enemy by
offering him an advantageous position.

Planning does not mean creating a rigid to-do list, but constantly rethinking what the situation demands.

Some managers are unable to change their approach to find an opportunity.
They might know the nature of their situation.
Still, they are unable to discover their hidden opportunity.

Some managers do not know how to change their methods of operation.
They can see an opportunity.
Still, they are unable to adapt so that they can use it.

2 You must continuously improve your analysis.
You must adapt to your opportunities and problems.
You can change your methods and still create consistent and predictable results.
You must tackle one problem after another and solve them once and forever.

3 You can discourage your opponents by using their weaknesses against them.
You can keep potential malcontents distracted by keeping them busy.
You can control your rivals by giving them a different goal to pursue.

CHANGE:

Management warriors embrace change because they can respond more quickly than others.

You must make use of war. 4
Do not trust that the enemy isn't coming.
Trust your readiness to meet him by remaining patient.
Do not trust that the enemy won't attack.
Rely only on your ability to pick a place that the enemy can't
attack.

You can exploit five different faults in a leader. 5
If he is willing to die, you can kill him.
If he wants to survive, you can capture him.
He may have a quick temper.
You can then provoke him with insults.
If he has a delicate sense of honor, you can disgrace him.
If he loves his people, you can create problems for him.
In every situation, look for these five weaknesses.
They are common faults in commanders.
They always lead to military disaster.

[11]To overturn an army, you must kill its general.
To do this, you must use these five weaknesses.
You must always look for them.

✦ ✦ ✦

PREPARATION:

*The battlefield
always favors
the prepared.*

4 You must look ahead competitively.

Never pretend that problems won't arise.

Trust your skill to deal with them by preparing for problems.

Do not think that you won't meet challenges.

Instead, you must develop a position in the organization that others depend upon.

5 All managers have five potentially fatal weaknesses.

If they can accept failure, they will fail.

If they are just trying to survive, they are trapped.

Some managers overreact.

They rush into making mistakes.

If they are afraid of criticism, they fail to decide.

If they are too fond of their people, they create problems.

In every situation, look for these five weaknesses.

They are common faults in many managers.

They can lead you to disaster.

These weaknesses can destroy you and your organization.

You must know how to avoid these weaknesses.

You must always be aware of them.

FLAWS:

Unexpected change preys on the emotions.

Related Articles from *Sun Tzu's Playbook*

In chapter eight, Sun Tzu teaches us the need to constantly adapt to the situation. To learn the step-by-step techniques involved, we recommend the Sun Tzu's Art of War Playbook articles listed below.

1.8 Progress Cycle: the adaptive loop by which positions are advanced.

1.8.1 Creation and Destruction: the creation and destruction of competitive positions.

1.8.2 The Adaptive Loop: the continual reiteration of position analysis.

1.8.3 Cycle Time: the importance of speed in feedback and reaction.

1.8.4 Probabilistic Process: the role of chance in strategic processes and systems.

4.7.1 Command Weaknesses: the character flaws of leaders and how to exploit them.

5.2.1 Choosing Adaptability: choosing actions that allow us a maximum of future flexibility.

5.2.2 Campaign Methods: the use of campaigns and their methods.

5.2.3 Unplanned Steps: distinguishing campaign adjustments from steps in a plan.

5.3 Reaction Time: the use of speed in choosing actions.

5.3.1 Speed and Quickness: the use of pace within a dynamic environment.

6.0 Situation Response: selecting the actions most appropriate to a situation.

6.1 Situation Recognition: situation recognition in making advances.

6.1.1 Conditioned Reflexes: how we develop automatic, instantaneous responses.

6.1.2 Prioritizing Conditions: parsing complex competitive conditions into simple responses.

6.2 Campaign Evaluation: how we justify continued investment in an ongoing campaign.

6.2.1 Campaign Flow: seeing campaigns as a series of situations that flow logically from one to another.

6.2.2 Campaign Goals: assessing the value of a campaign by a larger mission.

6.3 Campaign Patterns: how knowing campaign stages gives us insight into our situation.

6.5 Nine Responses: the best responses to the nine common competitive situations.

6.7 Tailoring to Conditions: overcoming opposition using conditions in the environment.

6.7.1 Form Adjustments: adapting our responses based on the form of the ground.

6.7.2 Size Adjustments: adapting responses based on the relative size of opposing forces.

6.7.3 Strength Adjustments: how to adapt responses based on the relative strength of opposing missions.

Chapter 9

Armed March: Making Progress

This chapter serves as a guide to making progress in a project to grow or improve your area of responsibility. This long chapter addresses the challenges encountered when moving an organization into new competitive territory. Much of it is dedicated to correctly interpreting signs in the environment.

When you undertake a project, you face different types of challenges. The chapter's first section covers four different categories of territory and how to navigate them.

What are the rules for a successful project? Sun Tzu briefly addresses the need to control the high ground in whatever type of situation you encounter.

How can you avoid getting your project into trouble? The third section warns about the seasonal and hidden dangers inherent in exploring new territory.

You can diagnose problems from scant information. The fourth section explains various signs in the environment and how to interpret them.

You can also understand what people are thinking from their actions. In the long fifth section, Sun Tzu explains in detail how you can determine the condition and intentions of your opponents by interpreting their behavior.

When have you gone far enough in your project? Sun Tzu ends the chapter by describing how to know when you have gone as far as you can go in a new competitive arena and how you can regroup.

Armed March

Sun Tzu said:

Anyone moving an army must adjust to the enemy. 1
When caught in the mountains, rely on their valleys.
Position yourself on the heights facing the sun.
To win your battles, never attack uphill.
This is how you position your army in the mountains.

[6]When water blocks you, keep far away from it.
Let the invader cross the river and wait for him.
Do not meet him in midstream.
Wait for him to get half his forces across and
then take advantage of the situation.

[10]You need to be able to fight.
You can't do that if you are caught in water
when you meet an invader.
Position yourself upstream, facing the sun.
Never face against the current.
Always position your army upstream when
near the water.

TERRAIN:

Strategy teaches that all terrains have different forms and these forms dictate how you must respond.

Making Progress

THE MANAGEMENT WARRIOR HEARS:

1 In every organization, you must serve the customer.
Avoid costly commitments and make small improvements.
Keep your organization visible and accessible.
To tackle problems, never throw money at them.
This is how to make progress in expensive situations.

When a technology will limit you, avoid it.
Let your competitors invest in it and use time against them.
Don't compete on who has the latest technology.
Wait until a technology is well proven and then take
advantage of falling prices.

You need to be productive.
You can't if you are wrestling with technology
instead of serving your customers.

SITUATIONS:

Use technology to make your processes visible.
Never fight against technological trends.
Leverage the trends when implementing a tech-
nology.

*The dynamics
of situations
have different
"shapes." They
can be uneven,
fluid, uncertain,
or solid.*

¹⁵You may have to move across marshes.
Move through them quickly without stopping.
You may meet the enemy in the middle of a marsh.
You must keep on the water grasses.
Keep your back to a clump of trees.
This is how you position your army in a marsh.

²¹On a level plateau, take a position that you can change.
Keep the higher ground on your right and to the rear.
Keep danger in front of you and safety behind.
This is how you position yourself on a level plateau.

²⁵You can find an advantage in all four of these situations.
Learn from the great emperor who used positioning to
conquer his four rivals.

Armies are stronger on high ground and weaker on low. 2
They are better camping on sunny southern hillsides than
on shady northern ones.
Provide for your army's health and place men correctly.
Your army will be free from disease.
Done correctly, this means victory.

⁶You must sometimes defend on a hill or riverbank.
You must keep on the south side in the sun.
Keep the uphill slope at your right rear.

⁹This will give the advantage to your army.
It will always give you a position of strength.

You may have to implement a short-term solution.
Use it briefly and never leave it in place.
You will have problems with short-term solutions.
When you do, save what is working well.
Work toward a solid, long-term resolution.
This is how you make progress in the short term.

When conditions are stable, identify what can be improved.
Invest in visibility and internal infrastructure.
Make problems visible and protect what works.
This is how to make progress in stable situations.

You can make progress in any situation.
Learn from successful managers who have continually improved
their organizations.

2 Groups are stronger with cash and weaker without it.
You are better off with solid cash reserves than with forecasted
budget surpluses.
Keep your organization healthy by keeping it solvent.
Your organization will be free from debt pressure.
Do this correctly and you will be successful.

Sometimes you must take on debt.
Keep it minimal and keep it visible.
Use it to build infrastructure.

This will create opportunities for your organization.
Cash always gives you a position of strength.

Stop the march when the rain swells the river into rapids. 3
You may want to ford the river.
Wait until it subsides.

4All regions can have seasonal mountain streams that can
cut you off.
There are seasonal lakes.
There are seasonal blockages.
There are seasonal jungles.
There are seasonal floods.
There are seasonal fissures.
Get away from all these quickly.
Do not get close to them.

SEASONS:

Keep them at a distance.
Maneuver the enemy close to them.

The changing climate part of every strategic position means that positions continually change.

Position yourself facing these dangers.
Push the enemy back into them.

16Danger can hide on your army's flank.
There are reservoirs and lakes.
There are reeds and thickets.
There are mountain woods.
Their dense vegetation provides a hiding
place.
You must cautiously search through them.
They can always hide an ambush.

3 Stop making changes when technological change is rapid.
You may want to use an evolving technology.
Wait until it stabilizes.

All organizations have internal restrictions and boundaries that
limit capacity.
There are temporary resource limitations.
There are temporary cost limitations.
There are temporary information limitations.
There are temporary technological limitations.
There are temporary span-of-control limitations.
Always avoid these limitations.
Do not even get close to them.
Leave yourself plenty of capacity.
You want to limit only your problems.
Keep your eye on your problems.
Let others fall into them unaware.

Danger can hide at the edges of your organization.
Beware of habits and prejudices.
Beware of hidden assumptions.
Beware of established processes.
Complicated processes provide a hiding place
where waste.
You must examine everything carefully.
You don't want to be blindsided.

PATIENCE:

*Common
changes endan-
ger projects only
if you rush into
them without
realizing what is
happening.*

Sometimes, the enemy is close by but remains calm. 4
Expect to find him in a natural stronghold.
Other times he remains at a distance but provokes battle.
He wants you to attack him.

5He sometimes shifts the position of his camp.
He is looking for an advantageous position.

7The trees in the forest move.
Expect that the enemy is coming.
The tall grasses obstruct your view.
Be suspicious.

COMPETITION:

Competition is part of the competitive environment and must be analyzed as part of that environment.

11The birds take flight.
Expect that the enemy is hiding.
Animals startle.
Expect an ambush.

15Notice the dust.
It sometimes rises high in a straight line.
Vehicles are coming.
The dust appears low in a wide band.
Foot soldiers are coming.
The dust seems scattered in different areas.
The enemy is collecting firewood.
Any dust is light and settling down.
The enemy is setting up camp.

4 Some problems arise frequently arise and are tolerated.
You must understand that they are well entrenched.
Other problems are uncommon but get attention.
Don't let them draw away your resources.

Sometimes a problem's source seems to shift around.
Solving it forever presents a real opportunity.

Well-established processes become less consistent.
Expect that a change has occurred.
Some processes are hard to measure.
Distrust them.

EVALUATION:

Situations can tell you what they hold in store if you judge by what you see in the environment.

People start to leave.
Look for hidden problems.
Employees quit.
Expect unhappy surprises.

Notice expenses.
Expenses can rise quickly in a specific area.
A quick change is coming.
Expenses can rise generally across a broad area.
This means that the market is getting more competitive.
Cost increases can be scattered throughout the organization.
This means people are padding their budgets.
Expenses can increase slightly and then decrease again.
This means that you have problems under control.

Your enemy speaks humbly while building up forces. **5**
He is planning to advance.

3The enemy talks aggressively and pushes as if to advance.
He is planning to retreat.

5Small vehicles exit his camp first.
They move the army's flanks.
They are forming a battle line.

8Your enemy tries to sue for peace but without offering a
treaty.
He is plotting.

10Your enemy's men run to leave and yet form ranks.
You should expect action.

12Half his army advances and the other half retreats.
He is luring you.

14Your enemy plans to fight but his men just stand there.
They are starving.

16Those who draw water drink it first.
They are thirsty.

18Your enemy sees an advantage but does not advance.
His men are tired.

5 A problem may seem unimportant but keeps growing.
It will get serious.

People worry about a potential problem and prepare for it.
It will be minimal.

Sudden changes in the organization aggravate problems that
already exist.
You must address them.

Some problems recede in importance for a time but never go away
entirely.
They will arise later.

Some problems seem easily solved but reappear later.
You need to do more.

Don't solve problems only to create as many new ones.
This is a trap.

There are solutions that can't be implemented.
There are limits to resources.

Those installing systems tackle their own problems first.
This means everyone is needy.

There is an opportunity but people can't take advantage.
People are overworked.

²⁰Birds gather.
Your enemy has abandoned his camp.

²²Your enemy's soldiers call in the night.
They are afraid.

²⁴Your enemy's army is raucous.
The men do not take their commander seriously.

²⁶Your enemy's banners and flags shift.
Order is breaking down.

²⁸Your enemy's officers are irritable.
They are exhausted.

JUDGMENT:

You best judge your competitors' situation by what they and their employees do rather than what they say.

³⁰Your enemy's men kill their horses for meat.
They are out of provisions.

³²They don't put their pots away or return to their tents.
They are desperate.

³⁴Enemy troops appear sincere and agreeable.
But their men are slow to speak to each other.
They are no longer united.

³⁷Your enemy offers too many incentives to his men.
He is in trouble.

Customers come.
This means that you are ahead of the competition.

People only suggest improvement anonymously.
They are afraid.

Employees are undisciplined.
They don't take management seriously.

The organization reorganizes, shifting responsibility.
Its structure is endangered.

Managers are short-tempered.
They are overworked.

The organization starts selling assets.
Operations are unprofitable.

People fail to put things away or stay in their areas.
Expect them to resist changes.

People seem sincere and agreeable.
Nevertheless, they fail to communicate.
They do not see themselves as a team.

The organization must offer incentives to get work done.
It is in trouble.

ADVANTAGE:

In competitive situations, you need to take advantage of the problems that your competitors are having.

39Your enemy gives out too many punishments.
His men are weary.

41Your enemy first acts violently and then is afraid of your
larger force.
His best troops have not arrived.

43Your enemy comes in a conciliatory manner.
He needs to rest and recuperate.

45Your enemy is angry and appears to welcome battle.
This goes on for a long time, but he doesn't attack.
He also doesn't leave the field.
You must watch him carefully.

If you are too weak to fight, you must find more men. 6
In this situation, you must not act aggressively.
You must unite your forces.
Prepare for the enemy.
Recruit men and stay where you are.

6You must be cautious about making plans
and adjust to the enemy.
You must gather more men.

EXPANSION:

*Campaigns
into new areas
expand your
control but they
also spread your
resources over a
wider territory.*

The organization constantly needs to discipline its people.
It is under pressure.

Your opponents first attack you and then quickly try to make friends.
They are developing more resources.

Opponents suggest a compromise solution.
They are simply buying time.

People seem angry at changes and threaten to fight them.
They remain opposed but do what they are told.
Nevertheless, they never agree.
You must keep your eye on them.

6 If the work isn't getting done, you must hire more people.
However, you must not try to expand operations.
You must build your organization.
You must train your new people.
You must expand your resources and be patient.

You must plan carefully and work continually to improve the organization.
You must increase the expertise of your team.

PAUSING:

Avoid new responsibilities when your resources are stretched too thin to make new progress.

With new, undedicated soldiers, you can depend on them 7
if you discipline them.
They will tend to disobey your orders.
If they do not obey your orders, they will be useless.

⁴You can depend on seasoned, dedicated soldiers.
But you must avoid disciplining them without reason.
Otherwise, you cannot use them.

⁷You must control your soldiers with esprit de corps.
You must bring them together by winning victories.
You must get them to believe in you.

¹⁰Make it easy for people to know what to do by training
your people.
Your people will then obey you.
If you do not make it easy for people to know
what to do, you won't train your people.
Then they will not obey.

¹⁴Make your commands easy to follow.
You must understand the way a crowd thinks.

YOUR TROOPS:

*Your success
depends totally
on your ability to
train, motivate,
and manage
the people with
whom you work.*

✦ ✦ ✦

7 With new, untrained employees, you can depend on them if you tell them exactly what to do.
Otherwise, they will get confused.
If they are confused, they cannot be productive.

It is different with established, trained employees.
You must let them see for themselves what needs to be done.
If they can't, they aren't good employees.

You must lead your people by inspiring them.
You must unite them by making them successful.
They must believe in you.

Make it easy for your people to follow directions by training them well.
They will then do what is necessary.
If operations are difficult to understand, you won't be able to train people.
Then they will make mistakes.

Make your processes easy to understand.
You must understand how groups of people work.

PEOPLE:

The key to management is controlling how your people perceive their situation and your own.

Related Articles from *Sun Tzu's Playbook*

In chapter nine, Sun Tzu discusses the basics of recognizing conditions in new territory. To learn the step-by-step techniques involved, we recommend the Sun Tzu's Art of War Playbook *articles listed below.*

1.1.0 Position Paths: the continuity of strategic positions over time.

1.2.2 Exploiting Exploration: how competitive landscapes are searched and positions utilized.

2.1 Information Value: knowledge and communication as the basis of strategy.

2.1.1 Information Limits: making good decisions with limited information.

2.2.1 Personal Relationships: why information depends on personal relationships.

2.2.2 Mental Models: how mental models simplify decision-making.

2.2.3 Standard Terminology: how mental models must be shared to enable communication.

2.3 Personal Interactions: making progress through personal interactions.

2.3.1 Action and Reaction: how we advance based on how others react to our actions.

2.3.2 Reaction Unpredictability: why we can never exactly predict the reactions of others.

2.3.3 Likely Reactions: the range of potential reactions in gathering information.

2.3.4 Using Questions: using questions in gathering information and predicting reactions.

4.0 Leveraging Probability: making better decisions regarding our choice of opportunities.

4.3 Leveraging Form: how we can leverage the form of our territory.

4.3.1 Tilted Forms: opportunities that are dominated by uneven forces.

4.3.2 Fluid Forms: opportunities that are dominated by fast-changing directional forces.

4.3.3 Soft Forms: opportunities that are dominated by forces that create uncertainty.

4.3.4 Neutral Forms: opportunities where the terrain has no dominant forces.

4.4 Strategic Distance: relative proximity in strategic space.

4.4.1 Physical Distance: the issues of proximity in physical space.

4.4.2 Intellectual Distance: the challenges of moving through intellectual space.

Chapter 10

地 形

Field Position: Best Practices

The characteristics discussed in this chapter help you analyze your opportunities to improve your current practices. This chapter examines in detail the six characteristics, called field positions, that you can use to evaluate your situation, especially in terms of moving to a better situation.

All your existing practices can be categorized into six categories. Sun Tzu begins with a detailed description of the six types of field positions and how to utilize them.

What types of weaknesses does your operations have? In the second section, Sun Tzu lists the six flaws in organizations and how to diagnose them. Though it is not explained specifically in the text, each of these six flaws arises in and is amplified by the specific field position that corresponds to the order in which it is listed.

No part of your operation is fixed in stone. Sun Tzu examines the issues that you must consider in moving from one temporary position to another.

The key to developing best practices is your relationship with your employees. The fourth section addresses the proper way to provide leadership to your people as you lead them into new situations.

Management ultimately depends on the depth of your knowledge. In the final section of the chapter, Sun Tzu addresses the need to compare your relative field position with that of your opponent before choosing a course of action.

Field Position

Some field positions are unobstructed. 1
Some field positions are entangling.
Some field positions are supporting.
Some field positions are constricted.
Some field positions give you a barricade.
Some field positions are spread out.

IN THE FIELD:

*Strategy teaches
that you can
learn the true
nature of a
territory only
once you have
entered into it.*

7You can attack from some positions easily.
Other forces can meet you easily as well.
We call these unobstructed positions.
These positions are open.
In them, be the first to occupy a high, sunny
area.
Put yourself where you can defend your
supply routes.
Then you will have an advantage.

Best Practices

1 Some of your group's practices are open.
Some of your group's practices are entangling.
Some of your group's practices are best practices.
Some of your group's practices are proprietary.
Some of your group's practices create protective barriers.
Some of your group's practices are too slow.

You can improve some of your procedures easily.
Problems can arise from these changes as well.
These are open processes.
They offer no obstacles to improvement.
With these procedures, keep their results highly
visible.
Focus on protecting your sources of financing and
income.
They are then valuable processes.

OPPORTUNITY:

*There are six
different forms
of opportuni-
ties and each
requires the
appropriate
approach.*

[14]You can attack from some positions easily.
Disaster arises when you try to return to them.
These are entangling positions.
These field positions are one-sided.
Wait until your enemy is unprepared.
You can then attack from these positions and win.
Avoid a well-prepared enemy.
You will try to attack and lose.
Since you can't return, you will meet disaster.
These field positions offer no advantage.

[24]You cannot leave some positions without losing an advantage.
If the enemy leaves this ground, he also loses an advantage.
We call these supporting field positions.
These positions strengthen you.
The enemy may try to entice you away.
Still, hold your position.
You must entice the enemy to leave.
You then strike him as he is leaving.
These field positions offer an advantage.

[33]Some field positions are constricted.
Get to these positions first.
You must fill these areas and await the enemy.
Sometimes, the enemy will reach them first.
If he fills them, do not follow him.
However, if he fails to fill them, you can go after him.

You can improve some practices easily.

You cannot return to old methods after making changes.

These are entangling processes.

They give you one chance.

Wait until you are certain a new procedure will work.

You can then replace an entangling process successfully.

Avoid lack of preparation.

You can launch a new process and have it fail.

Since you can't go back, you create a nightmare.

These processes are problems.

You cannot improve some practices without creating more serious problems elsewhere.

Your competitors cannot improve on them either.

These are the best current processes.

These processes create value.

You may be tempted to try to change them.

You must keep them in place.

Let your competitors experiment with them.

You can then attack your competitors for changing.

These practices offer a clear advantage.

Some practices are proprietary.

You must patent them before the competition does.

You must protect yourself and await a challenge.

Your competitors may use them first.

If they protect these processes, don't try to copy them.

If competitors leave you an opening, you can copy them.

³⁹Some field positions give you a barricade.
Get to these positions first.
You must occupy their southern, sunny heights in order to
await the enemy.
Sometimes the enemy occupies these areas first.
If so, entice him away.
Never go after him.

⁴⁵Some field positions are too spread out.
Your force may seem equal to the enemy.
Still you will lose if you provoke a battle.
If you fight, you will not have any advantage.

⁴⁹These are the six types of field positions.
Each battleground has its own rules.
As a commander, you must know where to go.
You must examine each position closely.

Some armies can be outmaneuvered. 2
Some armies are too lax.
Some armies fall down.
Some armies fall apart.
Some armies are disorganized.
Some armies must retreat.

YOUR FORCES:

*The term
"forces" means
all elements
used against the
competition,
both personnel
and resources.*

⁷Know all six of these weaknesses.
They create weak timing and disastrous
positions.
They all arise from the army's commander.

Some practices create protective barriers.

You must establish these processes before competitors do.

You then must promote your procedures and await competitive attacks.

Sometimes competitors establish these processes first.

If so, wait for your competitors to change.

Do not duplicate these processes.

Some practices are too slow.

Your resources may be equal to those of your competitors.

Nevertheless, you will lose in a battle.

In competitive markets, slow cycles offer no advantage.

These are the six categories of business processes.

Each organization has its own methods.

As a manager, you must know your practices.

You must analyze each procedure carefully.

2 Some organizations can be outmoded.

Some organizations are stagnant.

Some organizations stumble.

Some organizations self-destruct.

Some organizations are chaotic.

Some organizations must downsize.

You must recognize these six weaknesses.

They put you out of synch and undermine every organization.

Your decisions create them.

PREDICTION:

If you know the weakness of any operation, you can accurately predict the problems that it is likely to have.

¹⁰One general can command a force equal to the enemy.
Still his enemy outflanks him.
This means that his army can be outmaneuvered.

¹³Another can have strong soldiers but weak officers.
This means that his army is too lax.

¹⁵Another has strong officers but weak soldiers.
This means that his army will fall down.

¹⁷Another has subcommanders that are angry and defiant.
They attack the enemy and fight their own battles.
The commander cannot know the battlefield.
This means that his army will fall apart.

²¹Another general is weak and easygoing.
He fails to make his orders clear.
His officers and men lack direction.
This shows in his military formations.
This means that his army is disorganized.

COMMAND:

Only one person makes the key decisions in an organization, thereby shaping it and creating any flaws.

²⁶Another general fails to predict the enemy.
He pits his small forces against larger ones.
His weak forces attack stronger ones.
He fails to pick his fights correctly.
This means that his army must retreat.

Some organizations may be competitive in the market.
Still, they let themselves fall behind.
These organizations will become outmoded.

Some employees are strong but have weak managers.
Their organizations will become stagnant.

Some managers are strong but their employees are weak.
Their organizations will wear down.

Some managers are excitable and undisciplined.
They each have their own agendas.
The chief executive cannot know their true priorities.
Their organizations will self-destruct.

Some chief officers are lazy and sloppy.
They fail to make their priorities clear.
Their managers and employees lack direction.
This shows in the organization's lack of focus.
Their organizations are chaotic.

Some managers fail to foresee competition.
They pit weak methods against stronger ones.
They pit poor practices against better ones.
They fail to pick their battles correctly.
Their organizations must downsize.

COMPETITION:

You must avoid opportunities that pit you against competitors who have superior resources.

³¹You must know all about these six weaknesses.
You must understand the philosophies that lead to defeat.
When a general arrives, you can know what he will do.
You must study each general carefully.

You must control your field position. 3
It will always strengthen your army.

³You must predict the enemy to overpower him and win.
You must analyze the obstacles, dangers, and distances.
This is the best way to command.

⁶Understand your field position before you meet opponents.
Then you will succeed.
You can fail to understand your field position and meet
opponents.
Then you will fail.

¹⁰You must provoke battle when you will certainly win.
It doesn't matter what you are ordered.
The government may order you not to fight.
Despite that, you must always fight when
you will win.

FORESIGHT:

*Once you can
quickly diagnose
a situation, you
know the appro-
priate response
when others
leave openings.*

¹⁴Sometimes provoking a battle will lead to
a loss.
The government may order you to fight.
Despite that, you must avoid battle when you
will lose.

You must understand all six of these faults.
You must understand the thinking that creates them.
When you face these situations, you must know what to do.
You must study each one carefully.

3 You must control your processes and procedures.
Sound practices always strengthen your organization.

You must foresee problems and how to eliminate them.
You must analyze capacities, mistakes, and limitations.
This is the best way to manage.

You must understand your practices before you have a problem.
Then you will advance.
You may fail to understand the procedures you are using and meet a challenge.
Then you will fall behind.

You fix a process when you know it can be improved.
You should wait for direction to make changes.
The organization may prefer not to change.
Still, you must always improve processes whenever you can.

FLEXIBILITY:

As you learn more about your procedures, you must be willing to adapt your plans accordingly.

Sometimes you cannot improve procedures successfully.
Your organization may desire a change.
Still, you must avoid changes that will not work.

[17]You must advance without desiring praise.
You must retreat without fearing shame.
The only correct move is to preserve your troops.
This is how you serve your country.
This is how you reward your nation.

Think of your soldiers as little children. 4
You can make them follow you into a deep river.
Treat them as your beloved children.
You can lead them all to their deaths.

[5]Some leaders are generous but cannot use their men.
They love their men but cannot command them.
Their men are unruly and disorganized.
These leaders create spoiled children.
Their soldiers are useless.

You may know what your soldiers will do in an attack. 5
You may not know if the enemy is vulnerable to attack.
You will then win only half the time.
You may know that the enemy is vulnerable to attack.
You may not know if your men have the capability of
attacking him.
You will still win only half the time.
You may know that the enemy is vulnerable to attack.
You may know that your men are ready to attack.
You may not, however, know how to position yourself in the
field for battle.
You will still win only half the time.

You must make improvements without wanting praise.
You must abandon failures without embarrassment.
The only goal is to serve the customer.
This is how you serve your organization.
This is how you ensure success.

4 Think of your employees as your children.
They will support you in difficult circumstances.
Train them with care and understanding.
They will serve you faithfully.

Some managers pay good wages but do not value their people.
They care about individuals but do not guide them.
Their employees are unhappy and confused.
These managers create bad employees.
Their people are useless.

5 You may know what your people do in your organization.
You must also know how they create value for customers.
If you don't, you have not done your job.
You can know how to create value for customers.
You must also know how to organize your people to create that value.
If you don't, you have not done your job.
You can know how to create value for customers.
You can know how to organize your people to do it.
You must also know exactly how to formulate the processes in your organization.
If you don't, you still have not done your job.

[11]You must know how to make war.
You can then act without confusion.
You can attempt anything.

[14]We say:
Know the enemy and know yourself.
Your victory will be painless.
Know the weather and the field.
Your victory will be complete.

✦ ✦ ✦

RELATIVITY:

Your qualities, both good and bad, are important only in comparison with your opponents' qualities.

You must know how to improve your practices.

You can then act with certainty.

You can compete anywhere.

We say:

Know your competitors and your organization.

Then success will be effortless.

Understand people's thinking and your processes.

Then your success is assured.

Synthesis:

Strategy acknowledges that you cannot know everything so you must master a few key factors.

Related Articles from *Sun Tzu's Playbook*

In chapter ten, Sun Tzu discusses the use of temporary positions in building relationships with voters. To learn the step-by-step techniques involved, we recommend the Sun Tzu's Art of War Playbook *articles listed below.*

2.3 Personal Interactions: making progress through personal interactions.

2.3.1 Action and Reaction: how we advance based on how others reaction to our actions.

2.3.2 Reaction Unpredictability: why we can never exactly predict the react of others.

2.3.3 Likely Reactions: the range of potential reactions in gathering information.

2.3.4 Using Questions: using questions in gathering information and predicting reactions.

4.5 Opportunity Surfaces: judging potential opportunities from a distance.

4.5.1 Surface Area: choosing opportunities on the basis of their size.

4.5.2 Surface Barriers: how to select opportunities by evaluating obstacles.

4.5.3 Surface Holding Power: sticky and slippery situations.

4.6 Six Benchmarks: simplifying the comparisons of opportunities.

4.6.1 Spread-Out Conditions: recognizing opportunities that are too large.

4.6.2 Constricted Conditions: identifying and using constricted positions.

4.6.3 Barricaded Conditions: the issues related to the extremes of obstacles.

4.6.4 Wide-Open Conditions: the issues related to an absence of barriers.

4.6.5 Fixed Conditions: positions with extreme holding power.

4.6.6 Sensitive Conditions: positions with no holding power on pursuing opportunities.

4.7 Competitive Weakness: how certain opportunities can bring out our weaknesses.

4.7.1 Command Weaknesses: the character flaws of leaders and how to exploit them.

4.7.2 Group Weaknesses: organizational weakness and where groups fail.

4.8 Climate Support: choosing new positions based on future changes.

4.9 Opportunity Mapping: two-dimensional tool for comparing opportunity probabilities.

Chapter 11

Types of Terrain: The Work Environment

Managers must evaluate the type of work environment they operate in and are creating. This chapter describes nine different situations that tend to evolve as an army penetrates ever more deeply into enemy territory. Each of these situations or stages of development dictates a specific response. Each of these situations also has a clear analogue in the work environment.

What type of work environment are you in? The chapter's first section describes the nine campaign stages and the specific tactical focuses that they demand.

How can you keep control of that environment? Sun Tzu describes how to keep opponents from organizing and how to defend against invasion.

Adversity can be good. The third section discusses the general management of people using adversity to bring them together.

Speed is the essence of war. Sun Tzu addresses how to prepare the right responses beforehand.

He then discusses the functions of a leader.

In the sixth section, Sun Tzu reviews the stages of a campaign, with an emphasis on troop or group psychology.

Sun Tzu then emphasizes knowledge and unity as the keys to a successful campaign, with a special emphasis on the ability to recover from initial setbacks.

The final section addresses the need to set the proper tone for a campaign at the very start.

Types of Terrain

GROUND:

Ground, territory, and terrain are all part of the same Chinese concept, **di**, *which also means situation and condition.*

SUN TZU SAID:

Use the art of war. 1
Know when the terrain will scatter you.
Know when the terrain is easy.
Know when the terrain is disputed.
Know when the terrain is open.
Know when the terrain is intersecting.
Know when the terrain is dangerous.
Know when the terrain is bad.
Know when the terrain is confined.
Know when the terrain is deadly.

[11]Warring parties must sometimes fight inside their own territory.
This is scattering terrain.

[13]When you enter hostile territory, your penetration is shallow.
This is easy terrain.

[15]Some terrain gives you an advantageous position.
But it gives others an advantageous position as well.
This will be disputed terrain.

The Work Environment

THE MANAGEMENT WARRIOR HEARS:

1 Use the skills of management.
Know when the work environment is divisive.
Know when the work environment is easy.
Know when the work environment is competitive.
Know when the work environment is open.
Know when the work environment is shared.
Know when the work environment is risky.
Know when the work environment is bad.
Know when the work environment is restricting.
Know when the work environment is do-or-die.

ENVIRONMENT:

*These nine
terrains explain
a logical
evolution that
projects go
through as they
develop.*

People must sometimes defend the quality of their
work within their work team.
This is a divisive work environment.

People can address problems with minimum
conflict.
This is an easy work environment.

Some work environments are very productive.
These environments also encourage contention.
These are competitive work environments.

[18]You can use some terrain to advance easily.
Others can advance along with you.
This is open terrain.

[21]Everyone shares access to a given area.
The first one to arrive there can gather a larger group than
anyone else.
This is intersecting terrain.

[24]You can penetrate deeply into hostile territory.
Then many hostile cities are behind you.
This is dangerous terrain.

[27]There are mountain forests.
There are dangerous obstructions.
There are reservoirs.
Everyone confronts these obstacles on a campaign.
They make bad terrain.

[32]In some areas, the entry passage is narrow.
You are closed in as you try to get out of them.
In this type of area, a few people can effectively attack your
much larger force.
This is confined terrain.

[36]You can sometimes survive only if you fight quickly.
You will die if you delay.
This is deadly terrain.

In some work environments, workers are very productive.
People feel free to criticize each other.
These are open work environments.

Everyone shares access to the same areas and resources.
Those who are better at cooperation will be more productive than others.
This is a shared work environment.

People can be very productive in solving problems.
In doing so, however, they can create enemies.
This is a risky work environment.

There are stupid rules.
There are foolish restrictions.
There are meaningless goals.
Everyone runs into these problems in the organization.
These are bad work environments.

In some organizations, there is little margin for error.
People are locked in once they make a decision.
A small mistake can create big problems for your whole organization.
These are restricting work environments.

Sometimes people can succeed only by moving quickly.
They will fail if they delay.
This is a do-or-die work environment.

39To be successful, you must control scattering terrain by avoiding battle.

Control easy terrain by not stopping.

Control disputed terrain by not attacking.

Control open terrain by staying with the enemy's forces.

Control intersecting terrain by uniting with your allies.

Control dangerous terrain by plundering.

Control bad terrain by keeping on the move.

Control confined terrain by using surprise.

Control deadly terrain by fighting.

Go to an area that is known to be good for waging war. 2 Use it to cut off the enemy's contact between his front and back lines.

Prevent his small parties from relying on his larger force.

Stop his strong divisions from rescuing his weak ones.

Prevent his officers from getting their men together.

Chase his soldiers apart to stop them from amassing.

Harass them to prevent their ranks from forming.

8When joining battle gives you an advantage, you must do it.

When it isn't to your benefit, you must avoid it.

CONTROL:

Each of the nine "terrains," "conditions," or "stages" demands a specific form of response.

10A daring soldier may ask:
"A large, organized enemy army and its general are coming.
What do I do to prepare for them?"

To find success in divisive environments, you must discourage any opposition.

In easy environments, encourage everyone to keep going.

In competitive environments, discourage internal battles.

In open environments, keep everybody working together.

In shared environments, encourage good partnerships.

In risky environments, support the most productive people.

In bad environments, change the rules.

In restricting environments, be creative.

In do-or-die environments, encourage your people to succeed.

2 Identify the most important area for productivity.

You must understand the flow of information between your customers and your organization.

Keep small problems from growing into larger ones.

Keep simple problems from growing into complex ones.

Prevent management problems from affecting employees.

Untangle problems to identify separate issues.

Change procedures to prevent problems from recurring.

If changing the environment benefits you, you must do it.

If changing the work environment hurts your organization, you must avoid it.

You may ask:

"I foresee that my team faces very difficult organizational challenge.

What can I do?"

DIVISION:

When defending against specific rivals, you must try to divide their focus, resources, and positions.

¹³Tell him:

"First seize an area that the enemy must have.
Then he will pay attention to you.
Mastering speed is the essence of war.
Take advantage of a large enemy's inability to keep up.
Use a philosophy of avoiding difficult situations.
Attack the area where he doesn't expect you."

You must use the philosophy of an invader. 3
Invade deeply and then concentrate your forces.
This controls your men without oppressing them.

⁴Get your supplies from the riches of the territory.
They are sufficient to supply your whole army.

⁶Take care of your men and do not overtax them.
Your esprit de corps increases your momentum.
Keep your army moving and plan for surprises.
Make it difficult for the enemy to count your forces.
Position your men where there is no place to run.
They will then face death without fleeing.
They will find a way to survive.
Your officers and men will fight to their utmost.

¹⁴Military officers who are committed lose their fear.
When they have nowhere to run, they must stand firm.
Deep in enemy territory, they are captives.
Since they cannot escape, they will fight.

There is an answer.
First, protect the most important parts of your organization.
Then your people will pay attention.
Mastering speed is the essence of competition.
Take advantage of a large competitor's inability to keep up.
Your philosophy should be to avoid problem situations.
Target areas that your competitor has overlooked.

3 You must have an aggressive management philosophy.
Concentrate your organization on being totally competitive.
This commits your people without pressuring them.

You must be productive to succeed in the market.
Only productivity can support your whole organization.

Take care of people and don't overwork them.
Sharing your organization's success verifies your vision.
Keep the organization moving and prepare for surprises.
Make it difficult for the opposition to evaluate you.
Make it difficult for your employees to leave.
They will then face adversity without quitting.
They will find a way to make it work.
Your managers and employees will give everything they have.

When people are committed, they lose their fear of failure.
When they have nowhere else to go, they stick it out.
Deeply involved in the competition, they are locked in.
When they cannot go elsewhere, they will fight.

[18]Commit your men completely.
Without being posted, they will be on guard.
Without being asked, they will get what is needed.
Without being forced, they will be dedicated.
Without being given orders, they can be trusted.

[23]Stop them from guessing by removing all their doubts.
Stop them from dying by giving them no place to run.

[25]Your officers may not be rich.
Nevertheless, they still desire plunder.
They may die young.
Nevertheless, they still want to live forever.

[29]You must order the time of attack.
Officers and men may sit and weep until their lapels are wet.
When they stand up, tears may stream down their cheeks.
Put them in a position where they cannot run.
They will show the greatest courage under fire.

Make good use of war. 4
This demands instant reflexes.
You must develop these instant reflexes.
Act like an ordinary mountain snake.
If people strike your head then stop them with your tail.
If they strike your tail then stop them with your head.
If they strike your middle then use both your head and tail.

Your people must be totally devoted to their customers.
Without being warned, everyone will defend your customers.
Without being asked, everyone will create value.
Without being pushed, they will devote their energy.
Without being directed, they will earn your trust.

Stop their second-guessing by making your commitment clear.
Avoid failure by leaving people no excuses.

Your people and managers may not be rich.
This isn't because they don't want to be wealthy.
They may all fail.
This isn't because they don't want to succeed.

You must establish firm deadlines and targets.
Your people will complain that they cannot meet them.
Even when they start, they will tell you that it's impossible.
Put them in a position where they have no choice.
They will find a way to make it work.

4 Make good use of management.
You must make decisions quickly.
You must develop the ability to decide quickly.
You should be able to act on instinct.
If you run into financial problems, respond with productivity.
If you have productivity problems, respond with financial strength.
Problems can occur anywhere; address them immediately.

⁸A daring soldier asks:
"Can any army imitate these instant reflexes?"
We answer:
"It can."

ADVERSITY:

*Strategically,
unity is strength,
and nothing
unites a force
more than being
threatened by a
common enemy.*

¹²To command and get the most out of proud
people, you must study adversity.
People work together when they are in the
same boat during a storm.
In this situation, one rescues the other just
as the right hand helps the left.

¹⁵Use adversity correctly.
Tether your horses and bury your wagons' wheels.
Still, you can't depend on this alone.
An organized force is braver than lone individuals.
This is the art of organization.
Put the tough and weak together.
You must also use the terrain.

²²Make good use of war.
Unite your men as one.
Never let them give up.

The commander must be a military professional. 5
This requires confidence and detachment.
You must maintain dignity and order.
You must control what your men see and hear.
They must follow you without knowing your plans.

You may question:

"Can I manage making such quick decisions?"

There is only one answer.

"You must!"

To unite and get the most out of good people, you must have a common enemy.

You must make everyone understand that you are all in the same boat.

All will pull together when your people realize that they are part of a team.

LEADERSHIP:

People readily follow courageous leaders with a clear vision who create a sense of shared mission.

Use adversity correctly.

Tie your people to the success of your organization.

Still, this isn't enough.

A team is stronger than individuals alone.

This is the art of teamwork.

Tie the best people with the weakest.

You must use best practices.

Make good use of competitive pressure.

Unite your people as one.

Never let them quit.

5 You must be a management professional.

This requires confidence and detachment.

You must maintain your leadership and focus.

You must control what your people see and hear.

They must believe you without knowing your plans.

[6]You can reinvent your men's roles.

You can change your plans.

You can use your men without their understanding.

[9]You must shift your campgrounds.

You must take detours from the ordinary routes.

You must use your men without giving them your strategy.

[12]A commander provides what is needed now.

This is like climbing high and being willing to kick away your ladder.

You must be able to lead your men deep into different surrounding territory.

And yet, you can discover the opportunity to win.

[16]You must drive men like a flock of sheep.

You must drive them to march.

You must drive them to attack.

You must never let them know where you are headed.

You must unite them into a great army.

You must then drive them against all opposition.

This is the job of a true commander.

[23]You must adapt to the different terrain.

You must adapt to find an advantage.

You must manage your people's affections.

You must study all these skills.

You must reinvent your people's job descriptions.

You can change your direction.

You must get the most out of people without them knowing it.

You must change your approach.

You must experiment with different techniques.

You must direct people without explaining your strategy.

You must provide exactly what your people need now.

You must be willing to go out on a limb and take a risk to be successful.

You must get your organization deeply involved with your customers.

This will uncover the opportunities that you need to succeed.

You must inspire people to work together.

You must challenge them to produce.

You must challenge them to improve.

You must never need to explain what your intentions are.

You must unite them into a team.

You must challenge them to beat the opposition.

This is the job of a true manager.

You must adapt to every competitive environment.

You must adjust your methods to succeed.

You must guide your people's emotions.

You must learn all these skills.

Always use the philosophy of invasion. 6
Deep invasions concentrate your forces.
Shallow invasions scatter your forces.
When you leave your country and cross the border, you must take control.
This is always critical ground.
You can sometimes move in any direction.
This is always intersecting ground.
You can penetrate deeply into a territory.
This is always dangerous ground.
You penetrate only a little way.
This is always easy ground.
Your retreat is closed and the path ahead tight.
This is always confined ground.
There is sometimes no place to run.
This is always deadly ground.

[16]To use scattering terrain correctly, you must inspire your men's devotion.
On easy terrain, you must keep in close communication.
On disputed terrain, you try to hamper the enemy's progress.
On open terrain, you must carefully defend your chosen position.
On intersecting terrain, you must solidify your alliances.
On dangerous terrain, you must ensure your food supplies.
On bad terrain, you must keep advancing along the road.
On confined terrain, you must stop information leaks from your headquarters.
On deadly terrain, you must show what you can do by killing the enemy.

6 You must always manage aggressively.
Commitment to a goal focuses your efforts.
Weak commitments dissipate your efforts.
When you identify a goal and commit to it, you must immediately take control.
This is always a critical environment.
You can sometimes choose different directions.
This is always a good environment for partnerships.
You can commit everything you have to success.
This is always a risky environment.
At the beginning, the investment is small.
This is always an easy environment.
Later, you can't go back and you have few choices.
This is always a restricting environment.
Eventually, you have no place else to go.
This is a do-or-die environment.

To succeed in a divisive work environment, inspire employee dedication.
In an easy work environment, maintain good communication.
In a competitive work environment, you must track everyone's progress.
In an open work environment, people must stand behind their work.
In a shared environment, people must work well with others.
In a risky environment, you must have plenty of reserves.
In a bad environment, you must get mistakes behind you.
In a restricting environment, you must protect the organization with visibility.
In a do-or-die environment, your people must prove themselves by overcoming any obstacle.

²⁵Make your men feel like an army.
Surround them and they will defend themselves.
If they cannot avoid it, they will fight.
If they are under pressure, they will obey.

Do the right thing when you don't know your 7 different enemies' plans.
Don't attempt to meet them.

³You don't know the position of mountain forests, dangerous obstructions, and reservoirs?
Then you cannot march the army.
You don't have local guides?
You won't get any of the benefits of the terrain.

⁷There are many factors in war.
You may lack knowledge of any one of them.
If so, it is wrong to take a nation into war.

¹⁰You must be able to control your government's war.
If you divide a big nation, it will be unable to put together a large force.

KNOWLEDGE:

Strategy teaches that you can replace investment of time and effort with more complete information.

Increase your enemy's fear of your ability.
Prevent his forces from getting together and organizing.

Make your people feel like a team.

Make them part of the organization and they will defend it.

When they are committed, they will work.

When they are threatened, they will follow your lead.

7 Do the right thing when you don't understand the work environment.

Don't try to negotiate with people.

What if you don't understand the capacities, boundaries, and limitations?

Then you cannot move the organization.

What if you lack information?

Then you cannot get the benefits of good practices.

There are many issues crtitical to management success.

What if you lack understanding of any one of them?

You must not lead an organization in a competitive market.

You must be able to control an organization to compete.

Prevent people from being overwhelmed by the volume of work by dividing it.

Increase your opposition's problems.

Prevent your opponents from joining together against you.

REEVALUATE:

Analysis must be repeated constantly as you reexamine the five key factors that define your position.

[14]Do the right thing and do not arrange outside alliances
before their time.
You will not have to assert your authority prematurely.
Trust only yourself and your self-interest.
This increases the enemy's fear of you.
You can make one of his allies withdraw.
His whole nation can fall.

[20]Distribute rewards without worrying about having a system.
Halt without the government's command.
Attack with the whole strength of your army.
Use your army as if it were a single man.

[24]Attack with skill.
Do not discuss it.
Attack when you have an advantage.
Do not talk about the dangers.
When you can launch your army into deadly ground, even if
it stumbles, it can still survive.
You can be weakened in a deadly battle and yet be stronger
afterward.

[30]Even a large force can fall into misfortune.
If you fall behind, however, you can still turn defeat into victory.
You must use the skills of war.
To survive, you must adapt yourself to your enemy's purpose.
You must stay with him no matter where he goes.
It may take a thousand miles to kill the general.
If you correctly understand him, you can find the skill to do it.

Do the right thing and don't compete by making partnerships with opponents.
Then you won't have to fight for leadership.
Trust yourself and your own resources.
This increases your opponents' uncertainty.
You may convince your opponents' allies to abandon them.
Then their opposition can collapse.

Working alone, you don't have to play politics.
You can change direction without approval.
Focus the entire energy of your organization.
Use your organization as a united force.

Compete with skill.
Don't expose your plans.
Be aggressive when you find an edge.
Don't advertise the risks.
You can get into bad situations and lose a battle, but you can still survive.
You can weaken the organization, but you can also learn from your mistakes.

Even a strong organization can get into trouble.
If you make bad decisions, you can still turn initial failure into success.
You must use your management skills.
In management, you must adapt completely to the situation.
You must keep up with the competition in every area.
It can take years to win recognition for your leadership.
If you understand the opposition, you can find a way to succeed.

Manage your government correctly at the start of a war. 8
Close your borders and tear up passports.
Block the passage of envoys.
Encourage the halls of power to rise to the occasion.
You must use any means to put an end to politics.
Your enemy's people will leave you an opening.
You must instantly invade through it.

[8]Immediately seize a place that they love.
Do it quickly.
Trample any border to pursue the enemy.
Use your judgment about when to fight.

[12]Doing the right thing at the start of war is like
approaching a woman.
Your enemy's men must open the door.
After that, you should act like a streaking rabbit.
The enemy will be unable to catch you.

BEGINNINGS:

The start of a campaign is a delicate time when you set the direction for the entire course of the campaign.

8 Take the right steps when starting to manage.
Protect your organization and cancel all past privileges.
Get control of the information flow.
Make it clear that you are the person in charge.
Put an end to all office politics.
Identify the critical customer problems that you should solve.
Quickly attack these problems.

Instantly take control of the work environment.
Waste no time.
Destroy old boundaries to solve customer problems.
Use your best judgment about what to change.

Success at the start of management comes from wooing your
people.
The opposition will eventually leave an opening.
When it does, you must act quickly.
Your opponents will be unable to catch up with you.

OPENINGS:

*You cannot
advance posi-
tions without the
cooperation of
others who leave
you the open-
ings you need.*

Related Articles from *Sun Tzu's Playbook*

In chapter eleven, Sun Tzu explains instant situation response. To learn the step-by-step techniques involved, we recommend the Sun Tzu's Art of War Playbook *articles listed below.*

6.0 Situation Response: selecting the actions most appropriate to a situation.

6.1 Situation Recognition: situation recognition in making advances.

6.1.1 Conditioned Reflexes: how we develop automatic, instantaneous responses.

6.1.2 Prioritizing Conditions: parsing complex competitive conditions into simple responses.

6.2 Campaign Evaluation: how we justify continued investment in an ongoing campaign.

6.2.1 Campaign Flow: seeing campaigns as a series of situations that flow logically from one to another.

6.2.2 Campaign Goals: assessing the value of a campaign by a larger mission.

6.3 Campaign Patterns: how knowing campaign stages gives us insight into our situation.

6.3.1 Early-Stage Situations: the common situations that arise the earliest in campaigns.

6.3.2 Middle-Stage Situations: how progress creates transitional situations in campaigns.

6.3.3 Late-Stage Situations: understanding the final and most dangerous stages of campaigns.

6.4 Nine Situations: the nine common competitive situations.

6.4.1 Dissipating Situations: situations where defensive unity is destroyed.

6.4.2 Easy Situations: recognizing situations of easy initial progress.

6.4.3 Contentious Situations: identifying situations that invite conflict.

6.4.4 Open Situations: recognizing situations that are races without a course.

6.4.5 Intersecting Situations: recognizing situations that bring people together.

6.4.6 Serious Situations: identifying situations where resources can be cut off.

6.4.7 Difficult Situations: recognizing situations where serious barriers must be overcome.

6.4.8 Limited Situations: identifying situations defined by a bottleneck.

6.4.9 Desperate Situations: identifying situations where destruction is possible.

6.5 Nine Responses: using the best responses to the nine common competitive situations.

6.5.1 Dissipating Response: responding to dissipation by the use of offense as defense.

6.5.2 Easy Response: responding to easy situations by overcoming complacency.

6.5.3 Contentious Response: responding to contentious situations by knowing how to avoid conflict.

6.5.4 Open Response: responding to open situations by keeping up with the opposition.

6.5.5 Intersecting Response: the formation of situational alliances.

6.5.6 Serious Response: responding to serious situations by finding immediate income.

6.5.7 Difficult Response: the role of persistence in responding to difficult situations.

6.5.8 Limited Response: the need for secret speed in limited situations.

6.5.9 Desperate Response: using all our resources in responding to desperate situations.

6.6 Campaign Pause: knowing when to stop advancing a position.

Chapter 12

Attacking With Fire: Attacking Cycle Time

As a manager, you can use the lessons in this chapter to leverage factors in your environment. The focus of these lessons is the problem of cycle time. As the pace of change increases, every manager must address the issue of speed. Although Sun Tzu uses this chapter to discuss a specific weapon, fire, its broader subject is using any weapon, with an emphasis on leveraging forces in the environment as weapons.

Where do you start thinking about reducing cycle time? Sun Tzu begins by describing the five specific targets for environmental attack. He also addresses the critical importance of timing in these attacks.

Speed carries its own dangers. The second section of this chapter emphasizes that the attack itself is less important than the response to it. An attack does not create an opportunity. It is the response to it that creates the opportunity.

How does technology relate to speeding cycle time? Water is Sun Tzu's metaphor for change. We use it to address issues of technology. Fire is his metaphor for weapons, especially environmental weapons. Here we use it as a metaphor for speeding cycle time. Sun Tzu briefly compares using fire and water as environmental weapons in the next-to-last section.

Managers cannot afford the luxury of emotion in choosing targets. Sun Tzu ends by discussing the need to control emotional responses in both undertaking and responding to attacks.

Attacking With Fire

FIRE:

Classical strategy describes the element of fire as a weapon and uses it as a metaphor for all weapons.

SUN TZU SAID:

There are five ways of attacking with fire. 1
The first is burning troops.
The second is burning supplies.
The third is burning supply transport.
The fourth is burning storehouses.
The fifth is burning camps.

7To make fire, you must have the resources.
To build a fire, you must prepare the raw
materials.

9To attack with fire, you must be in the right season.
To start a fire, you must have the time.

11Choose the right season.
The weather must be dry.

13Choose the right day.
Pick a season when the grass is as high as the side of a cart.

15Choose the right time of day.
You want days when the wind rises in the morning.

Attacking Cycle Time

THE MANAGEMENT WARRIOR HEARS:

1 There are five ways to shorten cycle time:
First, you can speed production.
Second, you can speed supply.
Third, you can speed delivery.
Fourth, you can eliminate storage.
Fifth, you can speed communication.

To improve cycle time, you must have resources.
To make a change, you must prepare the new
procedures.

To improve quickness, you must synchronize processes.
To speed your cycles, you must take the time to do it.

Introduce changes during the right season.
People must have time to do what is needed.

Introduce changes during the right time of the month.
Pick a time when there are fewer deadlines.

Introduce changes during the right hour.
Start in the morning when people are full of energy.

CREATION:

*You recreate
an industry by
destroying the
existing
elements that
are unnecessary
for the industry.*

Everyone attacks with fire. 2
You must create five different situations with fire and be able
to adjust to them.

3You start a fire inside the enemy's camp.
Then attack the enemy's periphery.

5You launch a fire attack, but the enemy remains calm.
Wait and do not attack.

7The fire reaches its height.
Follow its path if you can.
If you can't follow it, stay where you are.

REACTION:

The environment is unpredictable so you must always act based upon how situations develop rather than on your plans.

10Spreading fires on the outside of camp can
kill.
You can't always get fire inside the enemy's
camp.
Take your time in spreading it.

13Set the fire when the wind is at your back.
Don't attack into the wind.
Daytime winds last a long time.
Night winds fade quickly.

17Every army must know how to adjust to the five possible
attacks by fire.
Use many men to guard against them.

2 All business cycles are speeding up.
You must master five different approaches to improve your cycle
time.

You can directly eliminate certain tasks.
To do this, change the processes around them.

If you eliminate a task, you may have no problems
at first.
Wait before making more changes.

The time a job takes expands.
Trace the history of time usage if you can.
If you don't understand it, avoid making changes.

Making small changes outside a process can work.
Don't always eliminate a task; speed it up.
Be patient in automating jobs.

Make time-cycle changes that other processes
support.
Don't save time in one place to lose it in another.
Visible time improvements last a long time.
Subtle ones fade quickly.

CONTROL:

*The less control
you have over
the way others
react, the more
control you must
have over the
way you react.*

You must master these five methods to improve your process cycle
time.
Ask your people to identify new ideas.

When you use fire to assist your attacks, you are clever. 3
Water can add force to an attack.
You can also use water to disrupt an enemy's forces.
It does not, however, take his resources.

You win in battle by getting the opportunity to attack. 4
It is dangerous if you fail to study how to accomplish this
achievement.
As commander, you cannot waste your opportunities.

[4]We say:
A wise leader plans success.
A good general studies it.
If there is little to be gained, don't act.
If there is little to win, do not use your men.
If there is no danger, don't fight.

[10]As the leader, you cannot let your anger interfere with the
success of your forces.
As commander, you cannot let yourself
become enraged before you go to battle.
Join the battle only when it is in your
advantage to act.
If there is no advantage in joining a battle,
stay put.

DECISIONS:

Your decisions must use the emotion of others. Your emotions cannot determine your decisions.

3 When you improve your cycle time, you always create value.
Technology can add force to change.

Using technology can eliminate problems.

It doesn't, however, always create value.

4 You succeed in any organization by innovating.
It is a mistake if you don't look for opportunities to improve process speed.

In management, you cannot waste any opportunity.

This much is true.

If you are smart, you plan to succeed.

If you are clever, you examine your organization.

If a change isn't worth the effort, don't attempt it.

If it can't make a difference, don't waste your efforts.

If there is no real problem, you can't solve it.

You must never let your emotions affect the success of your people.

You must never make changes simply because you are angry at individuals.

You need to meet only those challenges that are needed to make progress.

If there is no benefit in innovation, keep away from it.

SUCCESS:

A great innovative idea is not one that wins great recognition. It is one that makes a great profit.

[14]Anger can change back into happiness.
Rage can change back into joy.
A nation once destroyed cannot be brought back to life.
Dead men do not return to the living.

[18]This fact must make a wise leader cautious.
A good general is on guard.

[20]Your philosophy must be to keep the nation peaceful and
the army intact.

EMOTION:

Emotional grati-fication is never the goal of a competition. You must never lose sight of your goals in the heat of battle.

Something that upsets you now may one day make you happy.
Anger can lead to joy.
If you destroy the organization, there is no second chance.
Fired managers are not rehired.

Knowing this, you must be careful.
A good manager watches.

Your plan must be to keep the organization together and your people employed.

♦ ♦ ♦

THE PAYOFF:

Change is not a goal, but only the means to an end. Change only makes sense if it creates a stronger position.

Related Articles from *Sun Tzu's Playbook*

In chapter twelve, Sun Tzu discusses the use of environmental weapons. To learn the step-by-step techniques involved, we recommend the Sun Tzu's Art of War Playbook articles listed below.

9.0 Understanding Vulnerability: the use of common environmental attacks.

9.1 Climate Vulnerability: our vulnerability to environmental crises arising from change.

9.1.1 Climate Rivals: how changing conditions create opponents.

9.1.2 Threat Development: how changing conditions create environmental threats.

9.2 Points of Vulnerability: our points of vulnerability during an environmental crisis.

9.2.1 Personnel Risk: the vulnerability of key individuals.

9.2.2 Immediate Resource Risk: the vulnerability of the resources required for immediate use.

9.2.3 Transportation/Communication Risk: how firestorms choke normal channels of movement and communication.

9.2.4 Asset Risk: the threats to our fixed assets.

9.2.5 Organizational Risk: targeting the roles and responsibilities within an organization.

9.3 Crisis Leadership: maintaining the support of our supporters during attacks.

9.3.1 Mutual Danger: how we use mutual danger to create mutual strength.

9.3.2 Message Control: communication methods to use during a crisis.

9.4 Crisis Defense: how vulnerabilities are exploited and defended during a crisis.

9.4.1 Division Defense: preventing organizational division during a crisis.

9.4.2 Panic Defense: preventing the mistakes arising from panic during a crisis.

9.4.3 Defending Openings: how to defend openings created by a crisis.

9.4.4 Defending Alliances: dealing with guilt by association.

9.4.5 Defensive Balance: using short-term conditions to tip the balance in a crisis.

9.5 Crisis Exploitation: how to successfully use an opponent's crisis.

9.5.1 Adversarial Opportunities: how our opponents' crises can create opportunities.

9.5.2 Avoiding Emotion: the danger of exploiting environmental vulnerabilities for purely emotion reasons.

9.6 Constant Vigilance: where to focus our attention to preserve our positions.

Chapter 13

用 間

Using Spies: Acquiring Information

Although a manager doesn't (usually) employ spies as such, the lessons in this chapter about developing and using information sources are invaluable. In this last chapter, Sun Tzu addresses what he considers to be the most important element of strategy: information. A number of earlier chapters address the importance of information in their closing sections; here, in the closing chapter, Sun Tzu returns to that topic with a special emphasis on developing sources of information.

Information is money. Sun Tzu begins by describing the many costs of war that can be minimized by the right information. He makes the point that this information must come from people. To get good information, a manager must cultivate sources.

What types of information does a manager need? Sun Tzu lists the five different types of information and information sources.

Managing information is challenging. The third section discusses techniques for evaluating information and managing information sources.

What do you do when you have a specific project? The chapter's fourth section makes the point that before you tackle a specific problem you must first find sources that provide a complete picture of that problem.

Management is based on best practices. The closing section points out that the history of competition shows that success depends first on the cultivation of good information sources.

Using Spies

All successful armies require thousands of men. 1
They invade and march thousands of miles.
Whole families are destroyed.
Other families must be heavily taxed.
Every day, a large amount of money must be spent.

⁶Internal and external events force people to move.
They are unable to work while on the road.
They are unable to find and hold a useful job.
This affects 70 percent of thousands of families.

¹⁰You can watch and guard for years.
Then a single battle can determine victory in a day.

ECONOMICS:

The science of strategy is based on the idea that better information can be used to eliminate other costs.

Despite this, bureaucrats worship the value of their salary money too dearly.
They remain ignorant of the enemy's condition.
The result is cruel.

Acquiring Information

THE MANAGEMENT WARRIOR HEARS:

1 Making your team successful involves lots of other people.
People labor and work thousands of hours.
They invest a large part of their lives.
Many invest their hard-earned money.
Every day, organizations consume financial resources.

Internal and external events force people to change jobs.
Productivity is lost as they search for work.
Many are unable to find and hold good jobs.
Most people have been unemployed at some time.

You can manage an organization for years.
Then a single opportunity can determine your
team's success in a day.
Despite this, too many managers invest their
money primarily in salaries.
Investing too little in training, they are ignorant of
business changes.
The result is devastating.

INTELLIGENCE:

*Industries are
always
dominated by
companies that
are really in
touch with what
is changing.*

[15]They are not leaders of men.

They are not servants of the state.

They are not masters of victory.

[18]You need a creative leader and a worthy commander.

You must move your troops to the right places to beat others.

You must accomplish your attack and escape unharmed.

This requires foreknowledge.

You can obtain foreknowledge.

You can't get it from demons or spirits.

You can't see it from professional experience.

You can't check it with analysis.

You can only get it from other people.

You must always know the enemy's situation.

You must use five types of spies. 2

You need local spies.

You need inside spies.

You need double agents.

You need doomed spies.

You need surviving spies.

NETWORKS:

The key to gathering useful information is to have a range of different types of sources in your network.

[7]You need all five types of spies.

No one must discover your methods.

You will then be able to put together a true picture.

This is the commander's most valuable resource.

Without information, you cannot manage.
You cannot support your organization.
You cannot be successful.

You must be a creative and productive manager.
You must put your resources in the right places to be productive.
You must survive in a competitive environment.
This requires information.
You can get this information.
You won't get it from theory.
You won't get it from past experience.
You can't reason it out.
You can get it only by collecting it from other people.
You must always know your organization's condition.

2 You must use five types of information.
You need process information.
You need personnel information.
You need competitor information.
You need market information.
You need customer information.

You must use all five types of information.
If you do, no one can challenge your knowledge.
You can monitor your organization and its workings.
Information is your most valuable management resource.

INDIVIDUALS:

You need to build personal relationships to get the intelligence that makes a competitive difference.

[11]You need local spies.
Get them by hiring people from the countryside.

[13]You need inside spies.
Win them by subverting government officials.

[15]You need double agents.
Discover enemy agents and convert them.

[17]You need doomed spies.
Deceive professionals into being captured.
Let them know your orders.
They then take those orders to your enemy.

[21]You need surviving spies.
Someone must return with a report.

Your job is to build a complete army. **3**
No relations are as intimate as the ones with spies.
No rewards are too generous for spies.
No work is as secret as that of spies.

[5]If you aren't clever and wise, you can't use spies.
If you aren't fair and just, you can't use spies.
If you can't see the small subtleties, you won't get the truth
from spies.

[8]Pay attention to small, trifling details!
Spies are helpful in every area.

You need information on your processes.
Win it by putting measuring systems into place.

You need information on your people.
Find out what people can do through regular evaluations.

You need information on competitive methods.
Hire people from other organizations and use them.

You need market information.
You need to know where to obtain the best prices.
Let the market know your needs.
Encourage bidding to decrease your costs.

You need customer information.
You must know what your customers think.

3 Your job is to develop a strong organization.
No resources are as critical as information sources.
No reward is too generous for good information.
No knowledge is as hard to win as timely information.

You must be smart enough to correlate data.
You must be open and unbiased to evaluate it.
If you aren't sensitive to subtleties, you won't find the truth in
information.

You must pay close attention to small details.
Information is helpful in every area.

[10]Spies are the first to hear information, so they must not spread information.
Spies who give your location or talk to others must be killed along with those to whom they have talked.

You may want to attack an army's position. 4
You may want to attack a certain fortification.
You may want to kill people in a certain place.
You must first know the guarding general.
You must know his left and right flanks.
You must know his hierarchy.
You must know the way in.
You must know where different people are stationed.
You must demand this information from your spies.

[10]You want to know the enemy spies in order to convert them into your men.
You must find sources of information and bribe them.
You must bring them in with you.
You must obtain them as double agents and use them as your emissaries.

[14]Do this correctly and carefully.
You can contact both local and inside spies and obtain their support.
Do this correctly and carefully.
You create doomed spies by deceiving professionals.
You can use them to give false information.
Do this correctly and carefully.
You must have surviving spies capable of bringing you information at the right time.

Your people must gather information, but they must not spread it outside your team.

People who divulge your processes or plans to opponents will undermine you.

4 You may want to copy your competitors' best practices.
You may want to create a new department.
You may want to close an existing department.
You must first know how the opposition thinks.
You must know how others are organized.
You must know unofficial hierarchies.
You must know where opportunities are.
You must know where people want to work.
You must get this information from people.

You want to know who understands your competitors' best practices and hire them.
You must be willing to pay for information.
You must attract knowledgeable people to you.
You must win people with outside experience and use them to attract others.

You must do this carefully.
You can hire from your competitors if you want to win their knowledge.
You must also do this selectively.
You can discover purchasing information from the market.
You can use market competition to get better prices.
You must do this quietly as well.
You need detailed information on customer satisfaction as soon as possible.

[21]These are the five different types of intelligence work.
You must be certain to master them all.
You must be certain to create double agents.
You cannot afford to be too cost conscious in creating these double agents.

This technique created the success of ancient Shang. 5
This is how the Shang held their dynasty.

[3]You must always be careful of your success.
Learn from Lu Ya of Shang.

[5]Be a smart commander and a good general.
You do this by using your best and brightest people for spying.
This is how you achieve the greatest success.
This is how you meet the necessities of war.
The whole army's position and ability to move depends on these spies.

SOURCES:

Strategy is know how to leverage information sources.

There are five different types of information.
You must be certain to get access to them all.
You must be certain to understand competitive practices.
You cannot invest too much time in understanding the best practices.

5 This is how managers create successful organizations.
This is how they continue their success.

You must always be careful of your success.
Learn from the history of success.

You must be an informed and capable manager.
You must use your best and brightest people to gather information.
This is how you achieve the greatest success.
This is how you satisfy the needs of the organization.
Your management practices and ability to produce depend on information.

SUCCESS:

*Success is based
only on access
to superior
information.*

Related Articles from *Sun Tzu's Playbook*

In his final chapter, Sun Tzu explains how to use information channels. To learn the step-by-step techniques involved, we recommend the Sun Tzu's Art of War Playbook articles listed below.

2.0.0 Developing Perspective: adding depth to competitive analysis.

2.1 Information Value: knowledge and communication as the basis of strategy.

2.1.1 Information Limits: making good decisions with limited information.

2.1.3 Strategic Deception: misinformation and disinformation in competition.

2.1.4 Surprise: how the creation of surprise depends on the nature of information.

2.2 Information Gathering: gathering competitive information.

2.2.1 Personal Relationships: why information depends on personal relationships.

2.2.3 Standard Terminology: how mental models must be shared to enable communication.

2.3 Personal Interactions: making progress through personal interactions.

2.3.4 Using Questions: using questions in gathering information and predicting reactions.

2.3.5 Infinite Loops: predicting reactions on the basis of the "you-know-that-I-know-that-you-know" problem.

2.3.6 Promises and Threats: the use of promises and threats as strategic moves.

2.4 Contact Networks: the range of contacts needed to create perspective.

2.4.1 Ground Perspective: getting information on a new competitive arena.

2.4.2 Climate Perspective: getting perspective on temporary external conditions.

2.4.3 Command Perspective: developing sources for understanding decision-makers.

2.4.4 Methods Perspective: developing contacts who understand best practices.

2.4.5 Mission Perspective: how we develop and use a perspective on motivation.

2.5 The Big Picture: building big-picture strategic awareness.

2.6 Knowledge Leverage: getting competitive value out of knowledge.

2.7 Information Secrecy: defining the role of secrecy in relationships.

Glossary of Key Strategic Concepts

This glossary is keyed to the most common English words used in the translation of *The Art of War*. Those terms only capture the strategic concepts generally. Though translated as English nouns, verbs, adverbs, or adjectives, the Chinese characters on which they are based are totally conceptual, not parts of speech. For example, the character for CONFLICT is translated as the noun "conflict," as the verb "fight," and as the adjective "disputed." Ancient written Chinese was a conceptual language, not a spoken one. More like mathematical terms, these concepts are primarily defined by the strict structure of their relationships with other concepts. The Chinese names shown in parentheses with the characters are primarily based on Pinyin, but we occasionally use Cantonese terms to make each term unique.

ADVANCE (JEUN 進): to move into new GROUND; to expand your POSITION; to move forward in a campaign; the opposite of FLEE.

ADVANTAGE, *benefit* (LI 利): an opportunity arising from having a better POSITION relative to an ENEMY; an opening left by an ENEMY; a STRENGTH that matches against an ENEMY'S WEAKNESS; where fullness meets emptiness; a desirable characteristic of a strategic POSITION.

AIM, *vision, foresee* (JIAN 見): FOCUS on a specific ADVANTAGE, opening, or opportunity; predicting movements of an ENEMY; a skill of a LEADER in observing CLIMATE.

ANALYSIS, *plan* (GAI 計): a comparison of relative POSITION; the examination of the five factors that define a strategic POSITION; a combination of KNOWLEDGE and VISION; the ability to see through DECEPTION.

ARMY: see WAR.

ATTACK, *invade* (GONG 攻): a movement to new GROUND; advancing a strategic POSITION; action against an ENEMY in the sense of moving into his GROUND; opposite of DEFEND; does not necessarily mean CONFLICT.

BAD, *ruined* (PI 圮): a condition of the GROUND that makes ADVANCE difficult; destroyed; terrain that is broken and difficult to traverse; one of the nine situations or types of terrain.

BARRICADED: see OBSTACLES.

BATTLE (ZHAN 戰): to challenge; to engage an ENEMY; generically, to meet a challenge; to choose a confrontation with an ENEMY at a specific time and place; to focus all your resources on a task; to establish superiority in a POSITION; to challenge an ENEMY to increase CHAOS; that which is CONTROLLED by SURPRISE; one of the four forms of ATTACK; the response to a DESPERATE SITUATION; character meaning was originally "big meeting," though later took on the meaning "big weapon"; not necessarily CONFLICT.

BRAVERY, *courage* (YONG 勇): the ability to face difficult choices; the character quality that deals with the changes of CLIMATE; courage of conviction; willingness to act on vision; one of the six characteristics of a leader.

BREAK, *broken, divided* (PO 破): to DIVIDE what is COMPLETE; the absence of a UNITING PHILOSOPHY; the opposite of UNITY.

CALCULATE, *count* (SHU 數): mathematical comparison of quantities and qualities; a measurement of DISTANCE or troop size.

CHANGE, *transform* (BIAN 變): transition from one CONDITION to another; the ability to adapt to different situations; a natural characteristic of CLIMATE.

CHAOS, *disorder* (JUAN 亂): CONDITIONS that cannot be FORESEEN; the natural state of confusion arising from BATTLE; one of six weaknesses of an organization; the opposite of CONTROL.

CLAIM, *position, form* (XING 形): to use the GROUND; a shape or specific condition of GROUND; the GROUND that you CONTROL; to use the benefits of the GROUND; the formations of troops; one of the four key skills in making progress.

CLIMATE, *heaven* (TIAN 天): the passage of time; the realm of uncontrollable CHANGE; divine providence; the weather; trends that CHANGE over time; generally, the future; what one must AIM at in the future; one of five key factors in ANALYSIS; the opposite of GROUND.

COMMAND (LING 令): to order or the act of ordering subordinates; the decisions of a LEADER; the creation of METHODS.

COMPETITION: see WAR.

COMPLETE: see UNITY.

CONDITION: see GROUND.

CONFINED, *surround* (WEI 圍): to encircle; a SITUATION or STAGE in which your options are limited; the proper tactic for dealing with an ENEMY that is ten times smaller; to seal off a smaller ENEMY; the characteristic of a STAGE in which a larger FORCE can be attacked by a smaller one; one of nine SITUATIONS or STAGES.

CONFLICT, *fight* (ZHENG 争): to contend; to dispute; direct confrontation of arms with an ENEMY; highly desirable GROUND that creates disputes; one of nine types of GROUND, terrain, or stages.

CONSTRICTED, *narrow* (AI 狹): a confined space or niche; one of six field positions; the limited extreme of the dimension distance; the opposite of SPREAD-OUT.

CONTROL, *govern* (CHI 治): to manage situations; to overcome disorder; the opposite of CHAOS.

DANGEROUS: see SERIOUS.

DANGERS, *adverse* (AK 阨): a condition that makes it difficult to ADVANCE; one of three dimensions used to evaluate advantages; the dimension with the extreme field POSITIONS of ENTANGLING and SUPPORTING.

DEATH, *desperate* (SI 死): to end or the end of life or efforts; an extreme situation in which the only option is BATTLE; one of nine STAGES or types of TERRAIN; one of five types of SPIES; opposite of SURVIVE.

DECEPTION, *bluffing, illusion* (GUI 詭): to control perceptions; to control information; to mislead an ENEMY; an attack on an opponent's AIM; the characteristic of war that confuses perceptions.

DEFEND (SHOU 守): to guard or to hold a GROUND; to remain in a POSITION; the opposite of ATTACK.

DETOUR (YU 迂): the indirect or unsuspected path to a POSITION; the more difficult path to ADVANTAGE; the route that is not DIRECT.

DIRECT, *straight* (JIK 直): a straight or obvious path to a goal; opposite of DETOUR.

DISTANCE, *distant* (YUAN 遠): the space separating GROUND; to be remote from the current location; to occupy POSITIONS that are not close to one another; one of six field positions; one of the three dimensions for evaluating opportunities; the emptiness of space.

DIVIDE, *separate* (FEN 分): to break apart a larger force; to separate from a larger group; the opposite of JOIN and FOCUS.

DOUBLE AGENT, *reverse* (FAN 反): to turn around in direction; to change a situation; to switch a person's allegiance; one of five types of spies.

EASY, *light* (QING 輕): to require little effort; a SITUATION that requires little effort; one of nine STAGES or types of terrain; opposite of SERIOUS.

EMOTION, *feeling* (XIN 心): an unthinking reaction to AIM; a necessary element to inspire MOVES; a component of esprit de corps; never a sufficient cause for ATTACK.

ENEMY, *competitor* (DIK 敵): one who makes the same CLAIM; one with a similar GOAL; one with whom comparisons of capabilities are made.

ENTANGLING, *hanging* (GUA 懸): a POSITION that cannot be returned to; any CONDITION that leaves no easy place to go; one of six field positions.

EVADE, *avoid* (BI 避): the tactic used by small competitors when facing large opponents.

FALL APART, *collapse* (BENG 崩): to fail to execute good decisions; to fail to use a CONSTRICTED POSITION; one of six weaknesses of an organization.

FALL DOWN, *sink* (HAAM 陷): to fail to make good decisions; to MOVE from a SUPPORTING POSITION; one of six weaknesses of organizations.

FEELINGS, *affection, love* (CHING 情): the bonds of relationship; the result of a shared PHILOSOPHY; requires management.

FIGHT, *struggle* (DOU 鬥): to engage in CONFLICT; to face difficulties.

FIRE (HUO 火): an environmental weapon; a universal analogy for all weapons.

FLEE, *retreat, northward* (BEI 北): to abandon a POSITION; to surrender GROUND; one of six weaknesses of an ARMY; opposite of ADVANCE.

FOCUS, *concentrate* (ZHUAN 專): to bring resources together at a given time; to UNITE forces for a purpose; an attribute of having a shared PHILOSOPHY; the opposite of *divide*.

FORCE (LEI 力): power in the simplest sense; a GROUP of people bound by UNITY and FOCUS; the relative balance of STRENGTH in opposition to WEAKNESS.

FORESEE: see AIM.

FULLNESS: see STRENGTH.

GENERAL: see LEADER.

GOAL: see PHILOSOPHY.

GROUND, *situation, stage* (DI 地): the earth; a specific place; a specific condition; the place one competes; the prize of competition; one of five key factors in competitive analysis; the opposite of CLIMATE.

GROUPS, *troops* (DUI 隊): a number of people united under a shared PHILOSOPHY; human resources of an organization; one of the five targets of fire attacks.

INSIDE, *internal* (NEI 內): within a TERRITORY or organization; an insider; one of five types of spies; opposite of OUTSIDE.

INTERSECTING, *highway* (QU 衢): a SITUATION or GROUND that allows you to JOIN; one of nine types of terrain.

JOIN (HAP 合): to unite; to make allies; to create a larger FORCE; opposite of DIVIDE.

KNOWLEDGE, *listening* (ZHI 知): to have information; the result of listening; the first step in advancing a POSITION; the basis of strategy.

LAX, *loosen* (SHII 弛): too easygoing; lacking discipline; one of six weaknesses of an army.

LEADER, *general, commander* (JIANG 將): the decision-maker in a competitive unit; one who LISTENS and AIMS; one who manages TROOPS; superior of officers and men; one of the five key factors in analysis; the conceptual opposite of SYSTEM, the established methods, which do not require decisions.

LEARN, *compare* (XIAO 效): to evaluate the relative qualities of ENEMIES.

LISTEN, *obey* (TING 聽): to gather KNOWLEDGE; part of ANALYSIS.

LISTENING: see KNOWLEDGE.

LOCAL, *countryside* (XIANG 鄉): the nearby GROUND; to have KNOWLEDGE of a specific GROUND; one of five types of SPIES.

MARSH (ZE 澤): GROUND where footing is unstable; one of the four types of GROUND; analogy for uncertain situations.

METHOD: see SYSTEM.

MISSION: see PHILOSOPHY.

MOMENTUM, *influence* (SHI 勢): the FORCE created by SURPRISE set up by STANDARDS; used with TIMING.

MOUNTAINS, *hill, peak* (SHAN 山): uneven GROUND; one of four types of GROUND; an analogy for all unequal SITUATIONS.

MOVE, *march, act* (HANG 行): action toward a position or goal.

NATION (GUO 國): the state; the productive part of an organization; the seat of political power; the entity that controls an ARMY or competitive part of the organization.

OBSTACLES, *barricaded* (XIAN 險): to have barriers; one of the three characteristics of the GROUND; one of six field positions; as a field position, opposite of UNOBSTRUCTED.

OPEN, *meeting, crossing* (JIAO 來): to share the same GROUND without conflict; to come together; a SITUATION that encourages a race; one of nine TERRAINS or STAGES.

OPPORTUNITY: see ADVANTAGE.

OUTMANEUVER (SOU 走): to go astray; to be FORCED into a WEAK POSITION; one of six weaknesses of an army.

OUTSIDE, *external* (WAI 外): not within a TERRITORY or ARMY; one who has a different perspective; one who offers an objective view; opposite of INTERNAL.

PHILOSOPHY, *mission, goals* (TAO 道): the shared GOALS that UNITE an ARMY; a system of thought; a shared viewpoint; literally "the way"; a way to work together; one of the five key factors in ANALYSIS.

PLATEAU (LIU 陸): a type of GROUND without defects; an analogy for any equal, solid, and certain SITUATION; the best place for competition; one of the four types of GROUND.

RESOURCES, *provisions* (LIANG 糧): necessary supplies, most commonly food; one of the five targets of fire attacks.

RESTRAINT: see TIMING.

REWARD, *treasure, money* (BAO 賞): profit; wealth; the necessary compensation for competition; a necessary ingredient for

VICTORY; VICTORY must pay.

SCATTER, *dissipating* (SAN 攽): to disperse; to lose UNITY; the pursuit of separate GOALS as opposed to a central MISSION; a situation that causes a FORCE to scatter; one of nine conditions or types of terrain.

SERIOUS, *heavy* (CHONG 重): any task requiring effort and skill; a SITUATION where resources are running low when you are deeply committed to a campaign or heavily invested in a project; a situation where opposition within an organization mounts; one of nine STAGES or types of TERRAIN.

SIEGE (GONG CHENG 攻城): to move against entrenched positions; any movement against an ENEMY'S STRENGTH; literally "strike city"; one of the four forms of attack; the least desirable form of attack.

SITUATION: see GROUND.

SPEED, *hurry* (SAI 馳): to MOVE over GROUND quickly; the ability to ADVANCE POSITIONS in a minimum of time; needed to take advantage of a window of opportunity.

SPREAD-OUT, *wide* (GUANG 廣): a surplus of DISTANCE; one of the six GROUND POSITIONS; opposite of CONSTRICTED.

SPY, *conduit, go-between* (GAAN 間): a source of information; a channel of communication; literally, an "opening between."

STAGE: see GROUND.

STANDARD, *proper, correct* (JANG 正): the expected behavior; the standard approach; proven methods; the opposite of SURPRISE; together with SURPRISE creates MOMENTUM.

STOREHOUSE, *house* (KU 庫): a place where resources are stockpiled; one of the five targets for fire attacks.

STORES, *accumulate, savings* (JI 糧): resources that have been stored; any type of inventory; one of the five targets of fire attacks.

STRENGTH, *fullness, satisfaction* (SAT 壹): wealth or abundance or resources; the state of being crowded; the opposite of XU, empty.

SUPPLY WAGONS, *transport* (ZI 輜): the movement of RESOURCES through DISTANCE; one of the five targets of fire attacks.

SUPPORT, *supporting* (ZHII 支): to prop up; to enhance; a GROUND POSITION that you cannot leave without losing STRENGTH; one of six field positions; the opposite extreme of ENTANGLING.

SURPRISE, *unusual, strange* (QI 奇): the unexpected; the innovative; the opposite of STANDARD; together with STANDARDS creates MOMENTUM.

SURROUND: see CONFINED.

SURVIVE, *live, birth* (SHAANG 生): the state of being created, started, or beginning; the state of living or surviving; a temporary condition of fullness; one of five types of spies; the opposite of DEATH.

SYSTEM, *method* (FA 法): a set of procedures; a group of techniques; steps to accomplish a GOAL; one of the five key factors in analysis; the realm of groups who must follow procedures; the opposite of the LEADER.

TERRITORY, *terrain*: see GROUND.

TIMING, *restraint* (JIE 節): to withhold action until the proper time; to release tension; a companion concept to MOMENTUM.

TROOPS: see GROUPS.

UNITY, *whole, oneness* (YI 一): the characteristic of a GROUP that shares a PHILOSOPHY; the lowest number; a GROUP that acts as a unit; the opposite of DIVIDED.

UNOBSTRUCTED, *expert* (TONG 通): without obstacles or barriers; GROUND that allows easy movement; open to new ideas; one of six field positions; opposite of OBSTRUCTED.

VICTORY, *win, winning* (SING 勝): success in an endeavor; getting a reward; serving your mission; an event that produces more than it consumes; to make a profit.

WAR, *competition, army* (BING 兵): a dynamic situation in which POSITIONS can be won or lost; a contest in which a REWARD can be won; the conditions under which the rules of strategy work.

WATER, *river* (SHUI 水): a fast-changing GROUND; fluid CONDITIONS; one of four types of GROUND; an analogy for change.

WEAKNESS, *emptiness, need* (XU 處): the absence of people or resources; devoid of FORCE; the point of ATTACK for an ADVANTAGE; a characteristic of GROUND that enables SPEED; poor; the opposite of STRENGTH.

WIN, *winning*: see VICTORY.

WIND, *fashion, custom* (FENG 風): the pressure of environmental forces.

Index of Topics in *The Art of War*

This index identifies significant topics, keyed to the chapters, block numbers (big numbers in text), and line numbers (tiny numbers). The format is chapter:block.lines.

About the Author

Gary Gagliardi

This book's award-winning translator and primary author, Gary Gagliardi, is America's leading authority on Sun Tzu's *The Art of War*. A frequent guest on radio and television talk shows, Gary has written over wenty books on strategy. Ten of his books on Sun Tzu's methods have won award recognition in business, self-help, career, sports, philosophy, multicultural, and youth nonfiction categories.

Gary began studying Sun Tzu's philosophy over thirty years ago. His understanding of strategy was proven in the business world, where his software company became one of the Inc. 500 fastest-growing companies in America and won numerous business awards. After selling his software company, Gary began writing about and teaching Sun Tzu's strategic philosophy full time.

He has spoken all over the world on a variety of topics concerning competition, from modern technology to ancient history. His books have been translated into many languages, including Japanese, Thai, Korean, Russian, Indonesian, and Spanish.

Today he splits his time between Seattle and Las Vegas, living with his wife, Rebecca, and travels extensively for speaking engagements all over the world.

garyg@suntzus.com

@strategygary

Want to learn more about Sun Tzu's strategy?

SUNTZUS.COM

SCIENCE OF STRATEGY INSTITUTE

eBooks

Audio books

Audio seminars

Online training

Art of War and Strategy Books By Gary Gagliardi

Sun Tzu's Art of War Rule Book in Nine Volumes

Sun Tzu's The Art of War Plus The Art of Sales: Strategy for the Sales Warrior

9 Formulas for Business Success: the Science of Strategy

The Golden Key to Strategy: Everyday Strategy for Everyone

The Art of War Plus The Chinese Revealed

The Art of War Plus The Art of Management: Straegy for Management Warriors

Art of War for Warrior Marketing: Strategy for Conquering Markets

The Art of War Plus The Art of Politics: Strategy for Campaigns (with Shawn Frost)

Making Money By Speaking: The Spokesperson Strategy

The Warrior Class: 306 Lessons in Strategy

The Art of War for the Business Warrior: Strategy for Entrepreneurs

The Art of War Plus The Warrior's Apprentice: Strategy for Teens

The Art of War Plus Strategy for Sales Managers: Strategy for Sales Groups

The Ancient Bing-fa: Martial Arts Strategy

Strategy Against Terror: Ancient Wisdom for Today's War

The Art of War Plus The Art of Career Building: Strategy for Promotion

Sun Tzu's Art of War Plus Parenting Teens

The Art of War Plus Its Amazing Secrets: The Keys to Ancient Chinese Science

Art of War Plus Art of Love: Strategy for Romance

Printed in Great Britain
by Amazon

36277758R00127